The
ROCK & ROLL
ALMANAC

MARK BEGO

Macmillan • USA

In memory of Patty Meadows—
Rock & Roll never forgets

MACMILLAN
A Simon & Schuster Macmillan Company
1633 Broadway
New York, NY 10019-6785

MACMILLAN is a registered trademark of Macmillan, Inc.

Library of Congress Cataloging-in-Publication Data
Bego, Mark.
    The rock & roll almanac/Mark Bego.
        p.   cm.
    ISBN 0-02-860432-6 (alk. paper)
    1. Rock music—History and criticism.   2. Rock music—Miscellanea.   I. Title.
    ML3534.B43   1996   95-38561
    781.66—dc20   CIP
                                                                              MN

Manufactured in the United States of America
10 9 8 7 6 5 4 3 2 1

The author would like to thank the following:

Traci Cothran

Mike Goldberg/The Rock & Roll Hall of Fame

Jennifer Webb

Derek Burke

John Vasile

Fausto Bozza

Peter Max

Tony Seidl

Peter Schekeryk

Melanie

George Plentzas

Marcy MacDonald

Jack Cunningham

Sindi Markoff

Liz Derringer

Mark Sokoloff

Barbara Shelley

Martha Reeves

Mary Wilson

Contents

Introduction

I have always wanted to write my own rock & roll almanac, so I was thrilled to finally have this opportunity. In
my mind, an almanac of rock & roll has to be as bawdy,
as controversial, as exciting, as sexy, as silly, as outrageous, and as dramatic as rock musicians and rock
music itself. On top of that, it has to be as informative,
entertaining, and as fact filled as possible.

Well, to quote Alice Cooper, "Welcome to My Night-
mare!" On the pages of this book, I have toiled in a
fashion that would make "the hardest working man in
show business"—James Brown—proud. Under one
category or another, I have tried to include the names
and/or group names of every significant rock performer
of the 20th century (so far). Everyone from ABBA to ZZ
Top is somewhere on these pages, which spans the first
40 years, from Bill Hailey & His Comets in 1955 to Hootie
& the Blowfish in 1995.

Category-wise, I felt that *my* almanac had to truly
deliver the goods when it came to hard-core informa-
tion. Therefore, I've included every relevant rock & roll
Grammy Award winner; every rock birthday, rock death,
and rock drug overdose of major importance; every major
rock festival; as well as every inductee into the Rock &
Roll Hall of Fame and every winner of the Rhythm & Blues
Foundation's Pioneer Award. And, of course, there had
to be great gossip, which you'll find under headings
like "Who's Zoomin' Who?: The 10 Juiciest Rock & Roll
Scandals" and "The Chapel of Love: The Weirdest Rock

Marriages." Plus, there had to be rock bios on at least ten of the top rockers of all time.

I also believed that this book had to be just as loony as rock & roll itself. Any musical genre that could create hits like "Purple People Eater" and spawn groups with insane names like The Strawberry Alarm Clock and Toad the Wet Sprocket deserved special attention drawn to its total lunacy! I wanted this book to be insightful, dishy, automotive ("Drive My Car: Rockers' Automobiles"), outrageous ("Kind of a Drag: Best Cross-Dressing Displays by Rock Stars"), and at times a little tasteless ("I'm Gonna Hurl: Rock Stars Who Drowned in Their Own Vomit").

The section that took the most work was ultimately entitled "We Are the Champions: 14 of the Most Important Acts in Rock History." I originally wanted to present profiles of about 100 different rock stars, but I quickly realized that you can't zip through The Beatles' entire career in just two paragraphs. What I instead chose to do was to select 14 of the most original, most exciting, and best-loved stars, and tell their stories.

From a sales standpoint, The Beatles, The Supremes, Elvis, and Madonna have more Number One records than anyone else in musical history. For the other ten, I chose acts that displayed the greatest popularity, sales figures, and undeniable originality. I realize that not everyone is going to agree with my choices, but I guarantee that at least one of everyone's favorites is among my selection. (In other words, in the tradition of Leslie Gore's "It's My Party"—it's my book, and I wrote about who I wanted to!)

The section on the Grammy Award winners presented unique problems. In this book, I wanted to include all of rock's significant winners in all of the major categories. However, in several of the categories, such as Album of the Year, the early winners were decidedly un–rock oriented. I considered cutting all of the non-rock winners out of the listings, but then I chose to include them intact. Now you can see the exact spot in musical history when rock & roll overtook middle-of-the-road pop on the American music charts. The fact that Tony Bennett won the Album of the Year Grammy Award in 1994 only demonstrates how full circle music really is!

Unless otherwise noted, the record chart figures in this book are as per *Billboard* magazine's charts. Some of the hits and artists mentioned were more successful on the British charts, but references to those charts are specifically made. Also, for whatever reason, several of The Beatles' albums had different titles and configurations in England and in America. *Meet The Beatles* and *Magical Mystery Tour* were strictly American configurations. When the CDs were released in the 1980s in America, they were released in the original British configuration. My section on The Beatles refers to the original American vinyl albums and their performance on the American album charts at the time of their release.

Birthdays and awards are in calendar-date order, while the 14 rock star bios and "Rock Stars Who Died Too Soon" are in alphabetical order. The rest of the book was done "as I thought of it," for fear that every category would start with ABBA and end with ZZ Top.

I had a ball writing this book and coming up with as many off-the-wall categories as I could. I hope that you enjoy it. To paraphrase The Rolling Stones—I know it's only rock & roll, but I love it!

A Rock & Roll Chronology

JULY 11, 1951 Promoter/D.J. Alan Freed broadcasts his first R&B radio show at station WJW in Cleveland.

MARCH 21, 1952 When a riot breaks out at Alan Freed's Cleveland concert event, the Moondog Coronation Ball, the frenzied teenage musical excitement known as the Rock & Roll Era is officially under way.

SEPTEMBER 1952 The first edition of TV's "American Bandstand" is broadcast as a local show from WFIL-TV in Philadelphia, as "Bob Horn's Bandstand."

JANUARY 14, 1954 Alan Freed's live concert "Rock 'n' Roll Jubilee," held at the St. Nicholas Arena in New York City, is the first documented use of the term "rock 'n' roll." (Note: Since that time, rock music has been spelled "rock 'n' roll," "rock & roll," and "rock and roll.")

JULY 5, 1954 An ex–truck driver named Elvis Presley cuts his first single, "That's All Right Mama," for Sam Phillips's label, Sun Records.

JULY 9, 1955 Bill Haley & His Comets' "Rock Around the Clock" becomes the first rock & roll song to hit Number One.

JUNE 15, 1956 Paul McCartney meets John Lennon at a church picnic in Liverpool, England.

JULY 9, 1956   Dick Clark's first day of hosting "American Bandstand."

1956   Hollywood jumps in on the rock & roll trend sweeping the country, and six major rock films hit the screens. They are: *Don't Knock the Rock* (starring Bill Haley & His Comets, Little Richard, and Alan Freed), *The Girl Can't Help It* (starring Fats Domino, The Platters, Little Richard, Gene Vincent, and Eddie Cochran), *Rock Around the Clock* (starring Bill Haley & His Comets), *Shake, Rattle and Rock* (starring Fats Domino and Big Joe Turner), *Rock Pretty Baby* (starring Sal Mineo), and *Love Me Tender* (starring Elvis Presley).

AUGUST 5, 1957   "American Bandstand" begins a 30-year run as a nationally broadcast network show, starring host Dick Clark.

AUGUST 4, 1958   *Billboard* magazine christens its singles chart "The Hot 100."

FEBRUARY 3, 1959   A small plane crashes and kills Buddy Holly, Ritchie Valens, and the Big Bopper, making this the fabled "day the music died."

AUGUST 1, 1960   Aretha Franklin begins recording her first non-gospel album, with John Hammond producing for Columbia Records.

1961   Berry Gordy Jr. begins recording songs by local Detroit artists on a new label called Motown Records.

OCTOBER 26, 1962   The Motown Revue plays the first date of its three-month American tour in Washington, D.C., at the Howard Theater. The Revue includes Martha & the Vandellas, Marvin Gaye, The Supremes, Mary Wells, Smokey Robinson & the Miracles, "Little" Stevie Wonder, The Contours, The Temptations (backing up Wells), and The Marvelettes.

FEBRUARY 9, 1964   The Beatles make their first appearance on the TV variety program "The Ed Sullivan Show," and the '60s' "British invasion" of America's charts is under way.

APRIL 4, 1964   The Beatles claim the top five positions on *Billboard* magazine's "Hot 100" chart.

APRIL 26, 1964   The Rolling Stones release their self-titled debut album.

JULY 11, 1964   The Supremes' "Where Did Our Love Go" hits the "Hot 100" and goes on to become the first of five consecutive Number One hits released by the trio in less than a year, establishing The Supremes as the top female group in the world.

The "British Invasion" began when the Beatles stepped off of the plane in New York, in 1964.

SEPTEMBER 16, 1964   "Shindig" debuts on ABC-TV.

JANUARY 12, 1965   "Hullabaloo!" debuts on NBC-TV.

AUGUST 29, 1966   The Beatles play their final concert, at San Francisco's Candlestick Park.

SEPTEMBER 12, 1966   The first episode of "The Monkees" is broadcast on NBC-TV; the show and its stars are instant sensations, and The Monkees are labeled "the pre-fab four."

JUNE 16, 1967   The Monterey Pop Festival kicks off, starring The Mamas & the Papas, Janis Joplin, Jimi Hendrix, and The Who.

NOVEMBER 9, 1967   The first issue of *Rolling Stone* magazine is published.

APRIL 29, 1968   *Hair* opens on Broadway, at the Biltmore Theater.

JANUARY 17, 1969   Led Zeppelin releases its self-titled debut album, and ushers in "heavy metal" rock.

AUGUST 15, 1969 The Woodstock Music and Art Festival kicks off in Bethel, New York, at Max Yasgur's farm, starring Crosby, Stills, Nash & Young; Melanie; Sly & the Family Stone; Joan Baez; and Janis Joplin.

JANUARY 14, 1970 Diana Ross leaves The Supremes and the group successfully carries on without her.

DECEMBER 31, 1970 The Beatles officially break up.

MAY 25, 1974 "Rock the Boat," by the Hues Corporation, hits *Billboard*'s "Hot 100," and the disco era is officially under way.

APRIL 26, 1977 Studio 54 opens, with Cher and Bianca Jagger amongst the celebrities in attendance. The club goes on to become the ultimate night spot of the disco era.

AUGUST 16, 1977 Elvis Presley dies at his palatial estate, Graceland, after years of prescription-drug abuse.

DECEMBER 8, 1980 John Lennon is assassinated in New York City.

AUGUST 1, 1981 MTV begins broadcasting, and suddenly the rock & roll video network becomes *the* new way to promote a new artist or a new single.

JULY 13, 1985 The Live Aid concerts are held in London, England, and Philadelphia, Pennsylvania, as a charity event to help starving Africans.

JANUARY 20, 1986 The first induction ceremony of the Rock & Roll Hall of Fame is held at the Waldorf-Astoria in New York City.

1988 Compact discs officially outsell vinyl albums for the first time.

1991 Compact discs officially outsell audio cassettes for the first time.

JANUARY 11, 1992 Nirvana's album, *Nevermind*, hits Number One, and the grunge era is under way.

AUGUST 12, 1994 Woodstock '94 is held in Saugerties, New York, and Bethel '94 at Max Yasgur's farm; both kick off to celebrate the 25th anniversary of the original Woodstock festival.

DECEMBER 23, 1994 The double album *Live at the BBC* hits the *Billboard* charts and becomes the first new Beatles release in two decades.

FEBRUARY 25, 1995 Madonna becomes the female solo artist with the most Number One pop hits when her single "Take a Bow" reaches the top of the charts.

APRIL 4, 1995 The first Beatles single released in 25 years hits American stores, and the group again scores a Number One hit with "Baby It's You" from the *Live at the BBC* sessions.

SEPTEMBER 2, 1995 The Rock & Roll Hall of Fame Museum opens in Cleveland, Ohio. Bruce Springsteen, Aretha Franklin, Chuck Berry, Annie Lennox, Martha Reeves & the Vandellas, Little Richard, The Kinks, Melissa Etheridge, and dozens of top acts celebrate the event in concert.

The Inductees into the Rock & Roll Hall of Fame

1986

Performers

- Chuck Berry
- James Brown
- Ray Charles
- Sam Cooke
- Fats Domino
- The Everly Brothers
- Buddy Holly
- Jerry Lee Lewis
- Elvis Presley
- Little Richard

Non-Performers

- Alan Freed (*DJ/promoter*)
- Sam Phillips (*Sun Records president*)

Early Influences

- Robert Johnson
- Jimmie Rodgers
- Jimmy Yancey

Lifetime Achievement Award

- John Hammond

James Brown

1987

Performers

- The Coasters
- Eddie Cochran
- Bo Diddley
- Aretha Franklin
- Marvin Gaye
- Bill Haley
- B.B. King
- Clyde McPhatter
- Ricky Nelson
- Roy Orbison
- Carl Perkins
- Smokey Robinson
- Big Joe Turner
- Muddy Waters
- Jackie Wilson

Non-Performers

- Leonard Chess (*Chess Records president*)
- Ahmet Ertegun (*Atlantic Records co-founder*)
- Jerome Leiber (*songwriter*)
- Michael Stoller (*songwriter*)
- Jerry Wexler (*producer, Atlantic Records*)

Early Influences

- Louis Jordan
- Hank Williams
- T-Bone Walker

Performers

- The Beach Boys
- Bob Dylan
- The Beatles
- The Supremes
- The Drifters

Non-Performers

- Berry Gordy Jr. (*Motown Records president*)

Early Influences

- Woody Guthrie
- Les Paul
- Leadbelly

Performers

- Dion
- The Temptations
- Otis Redding
- Stevie Wonder
- The Rolling Stones

Non-Performers

- Phil Spector

Early Influences

- The Ink Spots
- Bessie Smith

- The Soul Stirrers

Performers

- Hank Ballard
- Bobby Darin
- The Four Seasons
- The Four Tops

- The Kinks
- The Platters
- Simon and Garfunkel
- The Who

Non-Performers

- Gerry Goffin (*songwriter*)
- Carole King (*award for her songwriting*)
- Lamonte Dozier (*songwriter/producer*)
- Eddie Holland (*songwriter/producer*)
- Brian Holland (*songwriter/producer*)

Early Influences

- Louis Armstrong
- Charlie Christian

- Ma Rainey

Performers

- Lavern Baker
- The Byrds
- John Lee Hooker
- The Impressions

- Wilson Pickett
- Jimmy Reed
- Ike & Tina Turner

Carole King

Non-Performers

- Dave Bartholomew (*arranger*)
- Ralph Bass (*songwriter/"Dedicated to the One I Love"*)

Early Performers

- Howlin' Wolf

Lifetime Achievement

- Nesuhi Ertegun (*Atlantic Records co-founder*)

1992

Performers

- Bobby Bland
- Booker T. & the MG's
- Johnny Cash
- The Jimi Hendrix Experience
- The Isley Brothers
- The Yardbirds
- Sam & Dave

Non-Performers

- Leo Fender (*developed the electric guitar*)
- Bill Graham (*promoter*)
- Doc Pomus (*songwriter*)

Early Influences

- Elmore James
- Professor Longhair

1993

Performers

- Ruth Brown
- Cream
- Creedence Clearwater Revival
- The Doors
- Etta James
- Frankie Lyman & the Teenagers
- Van Morrison
- Sly & the Family Stone

Non-Performers

- Dick Clark (*host/producer, "American Bandstand"*)
- Milt Gabler

Early Influences

- Dinah Washington

Performers

- The Animals
- The Band
- The Grateful Dead
- Duane Eddy

- Elton John
- John Lennon
- Bob Marley
- Rod Stewart

Non-Performers

- Johnny Otis

Early Influences

- Willie Dixon

Performers

- The Allman Brothers Band
- Al Green
- Janis Joplin
- Led Zeppelin

- Martha & the Vandellas
- Neil Young
- Frank Zappa

Non-Performers

- Paul Ackerman (*music editor,* Billboard, *1943–1973*)

Early Influences

- The Orioles

Performers

- David Bowie
- Jefferson Airplane
- Gladys Knight & the Pips

- Little Willie John
- Pink Floyd
- Velvet Underground

Recipients of the Rhythm & Blues Foundation's Pioneer Awards

1989

- LaVern Baker
- Charles Brown
- Ruth Brown
- Etta James
- Jimmy Scott
- Percy Sledge
- Mary Wells
- The Clovers

1990

No awards were given in 1990

1991

- Maxine Brown
- Ray Charles
- Al Hibbler
- Albert King
- Jimmy McCracklin
- Curtis Mayfield
- Sam Moore (Sam & Dave)
- Doc Pomus
- The Spaniels
- The Five Keys

- Aretha Franklin
- Hank Ballard
- Bobby "Blue" Bland
- Chuck Jackson
- Ella Johnson
- Paul "Hucklebuck" Williams
- The Dells
- The Staple Singers
- Rufus Thomas

- Hadda Brooks
- James Brown
- Solomon Burke
- Dave Clark
- Floyd Dixon
- David "Panama" Francis
- Lowell Fulson
- Erskine Hawkins
- Wilson Pickett
- Carla Thomas
- Jimmy Witherspoon
- "Little" Anthony & the Imperials
- Martha Reeves & the Vandellas

- Otis Blackwell
- Jerry Butler
- Clarence Carter
- Don Covay
- Bill Doggett
- Mabel John
- Ben E. King
- Johnny Otis
- Earl Palmer
- "Little" Richard Penniman
- Irma Thomas
- The Coasters (aka The Robins)
- The Shirelles

Gathered together for the 1995 Rhythm & Blues Foundation's Pioneer Awards are a who's who of the rock world: *(Left to right)* Mary Wilson (The Supremes), Inez Foxx, Bonnie Raitt, Fats Domino, Little Richard, Lloyd Price, Martha Reeves, Charlie Foxx, and Katherine Anderson (The Marvelettes).

1995

- Inez and Charlie Foxx
- Cissy Houston
- Illinois Jacquet
- Darlene Love
- The Marvelettes
- The Moonglows
- Lloyd Price

- Arthur Prysock
- Mabel Scott
- Booker T. & the MG's
- Junior Walker
- Justine "Baby" Washington
- Antoine "Fats" Domino

Every Elvis Presley Movie

1. LOVE ME TENDER

(20th Century Fox/1956)

Cast: Elvis Presley

                 Debra Paget

                 Richard Egan

                 Neville Brand

                 Mildred Dunnock

Director: Robert D. Webb

Hit Song: "Love Me Tender"

2. LOVING YOU

(Paramount/1957)

Cast: Elvis Presley

                 Lizbeth Scott

                 Wendell Corey

                 Delores Hart

                 James Gleason

Director: Hal Kanter

Hit Songs: "Teddy Bear"

                 "Loving You"

3. JAILHOUSE ROCK

(Metro-Goldwyn-Mayer/1957)

Cast:	Elvis Presley
	Judy Tyler
	Vaughn Taylor
	Dean Jones
	Mickey Shaughnessy
Director:	Richard Thorpe
Hit Songs:	"Jailhouse Rock"
	"Treat Me Nice"

4. KING CREOLE

(Paramount/1958)

Cast:	Elvis Presley
	Carolyn Jones
	Dolores Hart
	Dean Jagger
	Walter Matthau
	Paul Stewart
Director:	Michael Curtiz
Hit Song:	"Hard Headed Woman"

5. G.I. BLUES

(Paramount/1960)

Cast:	Elvis Presley
	Juliet Prowse
	Robert Ivers
	Leticia Roman
Director:	Norman Taurog

6. FLAMING STAR

(20th Century Fox/1960)

Cast:	Elvis Presley
	Barbara Eden
	Steve Forrest
	Dolores Del Rio
	John Mclntire
Director:	Don Siegel

7. WILD IN THE COUNTRY

(20th Century Fox/1961)

Cast:	Elvis Presley
	Hope Lange
	Tuesday Weld
	Millie Perkins
	John Ireland
	Gary Lockwood
Director:	Philip Dunne
Hit Songs:	"Wild in the Country"
	"Lonely Man"

8. BLUE HAWAII

(Paramount/1961)

Cast:	Elvis Presley
	Angela Lansbury
	Joan Blackman
	Iris Adrian
Director:	Norman Taurog
Hit Songs:	"Can't Help Falling in Love"
	"Rock-a-Hula Baby"

9. FOLLOW THAT DREAM

(United Artists/1962)

Cast:	Elvis Presley
	Arthur O'Connell
	Anne Helm
	Joanna Moore
	Jack Kruschen
Director:	Gordon Douglas

10. KID GALAHAD

(United Artists/1962)

Cast:	Elvis Presley
	Gig Young
	Lola Albright
	Joan Blackman
	Charles Bronson
Director:	Phil Karlson
Hit Song:	"King of the Whole Wide World"

11. GIRLS! GIRLS! GIRLS!

(Paramount/1962)

Cast:	Elvis Presley
	Stella Stevens
	Laurel Goodwin
	Jeremy Slate
	Ginny Tiu
Director:	Norman Taurog
Hit Songs:	"Return to Sender"
	"Where Do You Come From"

Elvis Presley in *It Happened at the World's Fair*

12. IT HAPPENED AT THE WORLD'S FAIR

(Metro-Goldwyn-Mayer/1963)

Cast:	Elvis Presley
	Joan O'Brien
	Yvonne Craig
	Gary Lockwood
	Ginny Tiu
Director:	Norman Taurog
Hit Songs:	"One Broken Heart for Sale"
	"They Remind Me Too Much of You"

13. FUN IN ACAPULCO

(Paramount/1963)

Cast: Elvis Presley

Ursula Andress

Paul Lukas

Alejandro Rey

Director: Richard Thorpe

Hit Songs: "(You're the) Devil in Disguise"

"Bosa Nova Baby"

14. KISSIN' COUSINS

(Metro-Goldwyn-Mayer/1964)

Cast: Elvis Presley

Arthur O'Connell

Glenda Farrell

Pamela Austin

Yvonne Craig

Director: Gene Nelson

Hit Song: "Kissin' Cousins"

15. VIVA LAS VEGAS

(Metro-Goldwyn-Mayer/1964)

Cast: Elvis Presley

Ann-Margret

Cesare Danova

William Demarest

Jack Carter

Director: George Sidney

Hit Songs: "Viva Las Vegas"

"What'd I Say"

16. ROUSTABOUT

(Paramount/1964)

Cast:	Elvis Presley
	Barbara Stanwyck
	Leif Erickson
	Joan Freeman
	Sue Ann Langdon
Director:	John Rich

17. TICKLE ME

(Allied Artists/1964)

Cast:	Elvis Presley
	Jocelyn Lane
	Julie Adams
	Jack Mullaney
	Merry Anders
	Connie Gilchrist
Director:	Norman Taurog
Hit Songs:	"It Feels So Right"
	"(Such an) Easy Question"

18. GIRL HAPPY

(Metro-Goldwyn-Mayer/1965)

Cast:	Elvis Presley
	Shelley Fabares
	Harold J. Stone
	Nita Talbot
	Mary Ann Mobley
	Jackie Coogan
Director:	Boris Sagal
Hit Song:	"Puppet on a String"

19. HARUM SCARUM

(Metro-Goldwyn-Mayer/1965)

Cast: Elvis Presley

Mary Ann Mobley

Ann Jeffries

Michael Ansara

Jay Novello

Billy Barty

Director: Gene Nelson

20. PARADISE, HAWAIIAN STYLE

(Paramount/1965)

Cast: Elvis Presley

Suzanna Leigh

James Shigeta

Donna Butterworth

Director: Michael Moore

21. FRANKIE AND JOHNNY

(United Artists/1966)

Cast: Elvis Presley

Donna Douglas

Harry Morgan

Sue Ann Langdon

Nancy Kovack

Director: Frederick de Cordova

Hit Songs: "Frankie and Johnny"

"Please Don't Stop Loving Me"

22. SPINOUT

(Metro-Goldwyn-Mayer/1966)

Cast: Elvis Presley

Shelley Fabares

Diane McBain

Deborah Walley

Cecil Kellaway

Una Merkel

Director: Norman Taurog

Hit Songs: "Spinout"

"All That I Am"

23. EASY COME, EASY GO

(Paramount/1967)

Cast: Elvis Presley

Dodie Marshal

Pat Preist

Elsa Lanchester

Frank McHugh

Director: John Rich

24. DOUBLE TROUBLE

(Metro-Goldwyn-Mayer/1967)

Cast: Elvis Presley

Annette Day

John Williams

Yvonne Romain

The Wiere Brothers

Chips Rafferty

Director: Norman Taurog

Hit Song: "Long Legged Girl (with a Short Skirt On)"

25. CLAMBAKE

(United Artists/1967)

Cast:	Elvis Presley
	Shelley Fabares
	Will Hutchins
	Bill Bixby
	Gary Merrill
Director:	Arthur Nadel

26. STAY AWAY, JOE

(Metro-Goldwyn-Mayer/1968)

Cast:	Elvis Presley
	Burgess Meredith
	Joan Blondell
	Katy Jurado
	Thomas Gomez
Director:	Peter Tewksbury
Hit Song:	"Stay Away"

27. SPEEDWAY

(Metro-Goldwyn-Mayer/1968)

Cast:	Elvis Presley
	Nancy Sinatra
	Bill Bixby
	Gale Gordon
Director:	Norman Taurog
Hit Songs:	"Let Yourself Go"
	"Your Time Hasn't Come Yet, Baby"

28. LIVE A LITTLE, LOVE A LITTLE

(Metro-Goldwyn-Mayer/1968)

Cast:	Elvis Presley
	Michele Carey
	Don Porter
	Rudy Vallee
	Dick Sargent
	Sterling Holloway
Director:	Norman Taurog
Hit Songs:	"Almost in Love"
	"A Little Less Conversation"

29. CHARRO!

(National General/1969)

Cast:	Elvis Presley
	Ina Balin
	Victor French
	Lynn Kellogg
	Barbara Werle
Director:	Charles Marquis Warren

30. CHANGE OF HABIT

(Universal/1969)

Cast:	Elvis Presley
	Mary Tyler Moore
	Barbara McNair
	Jane Elliot
	Leora Dana
	Edward Asner
Director:	William Graham
Hit Song:	"Rubberneckin'"

31. The Trouble with Girls

(Metro-Goldwyn-Mayer/1969)

Cast: Elvis Presley

Marlyn Mason

Nicole Jaffe

Sheree North

John Carradine

Vincent Price

Director: Peter Tewksbury

Hit Song: "Clean Up Your Own Back Yard"

32. Elvis: That's the Way It Is

(Metro-Goldwyn-Mayer/1970)

Cast: Elvis Presley

Kathy Westmoreland

The Sweet Inspirations

Director: Denis Sanders

33. Elvis on Tour

(Metro-Goldwyn-Mayer/1972)

Cast: Elvis Presley

J. D. Sumner and the Stamps

Directors: Pierre Adidge, Robert Abel

Hit Song: "Separate Ways"

Rock Stars with the Most Number One Hits

The Beatles   20

Elvis Presley   17

The Supremes   12

Michael Jackson   12

Madonna   11

Whitney Houston   10

Whitney Houston

The Weirdest Rock Marriages

Michael Jackson married to Lisa Marie Presley? Go figure!!!

MICHAEL JACKSON AND LISA MARIE PRESLEY (1994–   )

Jackson was still trying to weather the 1993 charges that he was having questionable liaisons with underage boys when it was announced that he had married Lisa Marie Presley, daughter of Elvis Presley. The mother of two children, and a recent divorcée, Lisa Marie is poised to inherit Elvis's entire legacy of cash and holdings. Although Lisa Marie is obviously a loving friend of Michael's, it is believed that this marriage was the "press release" union of the century.

DAVID BOWIE AND ANGELA BOWIE (1970–1980)

David Bowie's (Jones) marriage to Angela Barnet on February 20, 1970, was the most famous "open" marriage in rock & roll history. According to Angela, "When we first met, we were both laying the same bloke." During the years of their decade-long marriage, both publicly admitted being bisexual. Since their marriage legally ended in 1980, Bowie has denied a gender-bending period of his life. In the 1990s, after the divorce agreement "gag order" had lapsed, Angela promptly made the rounds of the TV talk shows, discussing intimate details of her union with Bowie, and how she once found him in bed with Mick Jagger. Their exploits were detailed in her sizzling 1993 autobiography *Backstage Passes*.

BILL WYMAN (THE ROLLING STONES) AND MANDY SMITH (1989–1992)

In 1984 Rolling Stones bass player Bill Wyman met a 13-year-old girl at the British Rock Awards and was immediately transfixed. With her parents' consent, he began dating Mandy Smith, but made certain that he was seen in public with women closer to his own age (48 at the time). The couple broke up when she was 16, and the story of Wyman being a "cradle robber" was the delight of the British tabloids. After two years, Bill and Mandy were again seeing each other. In 1989 the couple married when she was 18 and he was 52. Bill and Mandy's marriage was a disaster and ended in divorce in 1992. To twist the whole affair further, it was announced in 1993 that Bill's son, Stephen, was engaged to Mandy's mother—16 years his senior.

MADONNA AND SEAN PENN (1985–1989)

In 1985 Madonna, who was known as the Material Girl, was still enjoying her first year of international rock success when she met surly young "Brat Pack" actor Sean Penn. Problems with their romance became evident early on with their differing views of publicity: She loved having her photo taken wherever she went; he loathed the "celebrity" aspect of being a star. On several occasions during their four-year marriage, Sean publicly assaulted press photographers who shot photos of them on public streets, in cars, and in clubs. In 1988 Penn was put in jail for beating up a photographer, while Madonna was starring on Broadway in *Speed the Plow.* The marriage broke up a few months later when Madonna hinted at a lesbian affair with comedienne Sandra Bernhard. Since their divorce, Madonna's career has flourished, Penn's has floundered.

The Most Famous Rock Festivals

THE MONTEREY INTERNATIONAL POP FESTIVAL

Monterey, California / January 16–18, 1967
Attendance: 50,000

Acts included: The Mamas & the Papas, The Grateful Dead, Janis Joplin, Otis Redding, Jimi Hendrix, Canned Heat, Laura Nyro, Buffalo Springfield, Quicksilver Messenger Service, Ravi Shankar, Booker T. & the MG's, Hugh Masakela, Jefferson Airplane, The Who, The Association, The Electric Flag, The Paul Butterfield Blues Band, The Blues Project, Country Joe & the Fish

NEWPORT POP FESTIVAL

Costa Mesa, California / August 4–5, 1968
Attendance: 100,000

Acts included: The Byrds, Illinois Speed Press, Steppenwolf, Quicksilver Messenger Service, The Chambers Brothers, Tiny Tim, Iron Butterfly, The James Cotton Blues Band, The Paul Butterfield Blues Band

MIAMI POP FESTIVAL

Miami, Florida/December 28–30, 1968
Attendance: 99,000

Acts included: Fleetwood Mac, Buffy Sainte-Marie, Chuck Berry, Flat and Scruggs, Steppenwolf, Richie Havens, Sweetwater, Terry Reid, The McCoys, Pacific Gas & Electric, Marvin Gaye, Joni Mitchell, The Box Tops, Iron Butterfly, Jr. Walker & the All Stars, Joe Tex, The Grateful Dead, The Turtles, Ian & Sylvia

NEWPORT '69

Devonshire Downs, Northridge, California/June 20–22, 1969
Attendance: 150,000

Acts included: Ike & Tina Turner, The Rascals, Johnny Winter, The Byrds, Booker T. & the MG's, Eric Burdon, Taj Mahal, Jimi Hendrix, Creedence Clearwater Revival, Jethro Tull, Spirit, Joe Cocker

NEWPORT JAZZ FESTIVAL (SPECIAL ROCK LINEUP)

Newport, Rhode Island/July 3–6, 1969
Attendance: 78,000

Acts included: Jeff Beck; Led Zeppelin; Ten Years After; Blood, Sweat & Tears; James Brown; Jethro Tull

ATLANTA POP FESTIVAL

Atlanta, Georgia/July 4–5, 1969
Attendance: 110,000

Acts included: Chicago, Spirit, Joe Cocker, Creedence Clearwater Revival, Ten Wheel Drive, Delaney & Bonnie, Canned Heat, Ian & Sylvia, Johnny Winter, Led Zeppelin, The Staple Singers

ATLANTIC CITY POP FESTIVAL

Atlantic City, New Jersey/August 1–3, 1969
Attendance: 110,000

Acts included: Three Dog Night, Canned Heat, Little Richard, Santana, Jefferson Airplane, B.B. King, Booker T. & the MG's, Joni Mitchell, The Chambers Brothers, Dr. John, Iron Butterfly, Procol Harum, Janis Joplin, Arthur Brown

WOODSTOCK

The rock festival to end them all, held at Max Yasgur's farm.
Bethel, New York/August 15–17, 1969
Attendance: 400,000+

Acts included: Jimi Hendrix; The Who; Melanie; Country Joe & the Fish; Mountain; Tim Hardin; The Grateful Dead; Johnny Winter; John Sebastian; Ravi Shankar; The Paul Butterfield Blues Band; Ten Years After; Creedence Clearwater Revival; Blood, Sweat & Tears; Arlo Guthrie; The Band; Richie Havens; Sly & the Family Stone; Santana; Canned Heat; Sweetwater; Sha Na Na; Keef Hartley; The Incredible String Band; Joan Baez; Jefferson Airplane; Joe Cocker; Quill; Bert Somnier; Crosby, Stills, Nash & Young

TEXAS INTERNATIONAL POP FESTIVAL

Lewisville, Texas/August 30–September 1, 1969
Attendance: 120,000

Acts included: Janis Joplin, Johnny Winter, Rotary Connection, Sam & Dave, Grand Funk Railroad, Led Zeppelin, Delaney & Bonnie, The Incredible String Band, Nazz, Santana, Spirit, Sweetwater, Tony Joe White, Chicago

ALTAMONT

Livermore, California/December 6, 1969
Attendance: 300,000

Acts included: The Rolling Stones; Jefferson Airplane; The Flying Burrito Brothers; Santana; Crosby, Stills, Nash & Young

ATLANTA POP FESTIVAL

Byron, Georgia/July 3–5, 1970
Attendance: 200,000+

Acts included: Jimi Hendrix, Johnny Winter, Jethro Tull, Rare Earth, Mountain, Procol Harum, The Chambers Brothers, The Allman Brothers, Lee Michaels

MOUNT POCONO FESTIVAL

Long Pond, Pennsylvania/July 8, 1972
Attendance: 200,000

Acts included: Three Dog Night; The J. Geils Band; Humble Pie; Rod Stewart; Emerson, Lake & Palmer

NO NUKES (THE MUSE CONCERTS FOR A NON-NUCLEAR FUTURE)

Madison Square Garden, New York City/September 19–23, 1979
Attendance: 72,000 (18,000 per night/four nights)

Acts included: The Doobie Brothers; Bonnie Raitt; Jackson Browne; Carly Simon; James Taylor; Bruce Springsteen & the E Street Band; Tom Petty & the Heartbreakers; Nicolette Larson; Chaka Khan; Ry Cooder; Jesse Colin Young; John Hall; Gil Scott-Heron; Sweet Honey in the Rock; Raydio; Crosby, Stills & Nash

THE US FESTIVAL

San Bernardino, California/September 3–5, 1982
Attendance: 400,000

Acts included: Fleetwood Mac, Tom Petty, The Police, Jackson Browne, Pat Benatar, The Cars, Talking Heads, The Grateful Dead, The Kinks, The B-52's, Dave Edmunds, Santana, Eddie Money, Gang of Four, The Ramones, English Beat, Jerry Jeff Walker

THE US FESTIVAL '83

Southern California/May 28, 29, 30; June 4, 1983
Attendance: 725,000

Acts included: The Clash, Stray Cats, Men at Work, Judas Priest, Ozzy Osbourne, The Scorpions, Missing Persons, U2, The Pretenders, Stevie Nicks, Van Halen, David Bowie

LIVE AID

Philadelphia, Pennsylvania, and London, England, simultaneously, broadcast live/July 13, 1985
Estimated viewing audience: millions

Acts included: David Bowie; Paul McCartney; Alison Moyet; Sade; The Who; Elton John and Kiki Dee; Hall & Oates with David Ruffin & Eddie Kendricks; Mick Jagger; Tina Turner; Bob Dylan; Patti LaBelle; The Cars; The Beach Boys; Dire Straits; George Thorogood; Queen; Simple Minds; The Pretenders; Spandau Ballet; Santana; Ashford & Simpson; Teddy Pendergrass; Howard Jones; The Four Tops; Tom Petty & the Heartbreakers; Status Quo; Style Council; Boom Town Rats; Men at Work; Ultravox; Little River Band; Joan Baez; The Hooters; B.B. King; Billy Ocean; Billy Conoley; Nik Kershaw; Black Sabbath; Ozzy Osborne; Sting; Autograph; Bryan Ferry; Judas Priest; U2; Paul Young; Rick Springfield; Madonna; Phil Collins; Jimmy Page; Robert Plant; Duran Duran; Crosby, Stills, Nash & Young

BETHEL '94

Woodstock 25th Anniversary festival on the site of the original Woodstock festival, in Bethel, New York/August 12–14, 1994
Attendance: 30,000

Acts included: Melanie, Arlo Guthrie, Richie Havens

Melanie at Bethel '94—celebrating the 25th anniversary of Woodstock, at the original site where she made her "festival debut" in 1969.

WOODSTOCK '94

Saugerties, New York /August 12–14, 1994
Attendance: 300,000+

Acts included: Blues Traveler; Jakyl; Live; Sheryl Crow; Collective Soul; Candlebox; The Violent Femmes; Joe Cocker; The Cranberries; Blind Melon; Cypress Hill; The Rollins Band; Melissa Etheridge; Primus; Nine Inch Nails; Salt-n-Pepa; Metallica; Aerosmith; Traffic; Green Day; Paul Rodgers; Bonham; Neal Schon; Andy Fraser; Porno for Pyros; The Neville Brothers; Bob Dylan; Peter Gabriel; Crosby, Stills & Nash

(Left to right) David Crosby, Graham Nash, and Stephen Stills in 1994, amid their 25th anniversary tour, which included Woodstock '94.

Rock Stars with Their Own TV Shows

"THE MONKEES"

Network	NBC-TV
Airdates	September 12, 1966–August 19, 1968
Episodes	58

"THE PARTRIDGE FAMILY"

Network	ABC-TV
Airdates	September 25, 1970–September 7, 1974
Episodes	96

"THE SONNY & CHER COMEDY HOUR"

Network	CBS-TV
Airdates	August 1, 1971–May 29, 1974
Episodes	61

"THE SONNY COMEDY REVUE"

Network	ABC-TV
Airdates	September 22, 1974–December 29, 1974
Episodes	13

With and without Sonny, Cher has been the star of three different TV series.

"CHER"

Network	CBS-TV
Airdates	February 16, 1975–January 4, 1976
Episodes	26

"THE SONNY & CHER SHOW"

Network   CBS-TV

Airdates   February 1, 1976–March 18, 1977

"ROLLIN' WITH KENNY ROGERS & THE FIRST EDITION" (ALSO KNOWN AS "ROLLIN' ON THE RIVER")

Network   Syndicated

Airdates   1971–1972

Episodes   26

"THE BOBBY DARIN AMUSEMENT COMPANY"

Network   NBC-TV

Airdates   July 27, 1972–September 7, 1972

"THE BOBBY DARIN SHOW"

Network   NBC-TV

Airdates   January 19, 1973–April 27, 1973

"THE HELEN REDDY SHOW"

Network   NBC-TV

Airdates   June 28, 1973–August 16, 1973

"BOBBIE GENTRY'S HAPPINESS HOUR"

Network   CBS-TV

Airdates   June 5, 1974–June 26, 1974

Episodes   4

"TONY ORLANDO & DAWN"

Network   CBS-TV

Airdates   July 4, 1974–July 24, 1974; December 4, 1974– December 26, 1976

"THE HUDSON BROTHERS"

Network	CBS-TV
Airdates	July 31, 1974–August 28, 1974
Episodes	4

"THE HUDSON BROTHERS RAZZLE DAZZLE COMEDY SHOW"

Network	CBS-TV
Airdates	September 7, 1974–April 17, 1977
Episodes	24

"BONKERS" (HOSTED BY THE HUDSON BROTHERS)

Network	Syndicated
Airdates	September 1978–1979
Episodes	24

"GLADYS KNIGHT & THE PIPS"

Network	NBC-TV
Airdates	July 10, 1975–July 31, 1975
Episodes	4

"THE MANHATTAN TRANSFER"

Network	CBS-TV
Airdates	August 10, 1975–August 31, 1975
Episodes	4

"THE BOBBY VINTON SHOW"

Network	Syndicated
Airdates	1975–1978
Episodes	52

"DONNY & MARIE" (HOSTED BY DONNY AND MARIE OSMOND)

Network	ABC-TV
Airdates	January 23, 1976–January 19, 1979
Episodes	57

"THE JACKSONS"

Network	CBS-TV
Airdates	June 16, 1976–July 7, 1976; January 26, 1977–May 9, 1977
Episodes	12

"EASY DOES IT; STARRING FRANKIE AVALON"

Network	CBS-TV
Airdates	August 25, 1976–September 15, 1976
Episodes	4
Regular guest	Annette Funicello

"THE CAPTAIN & TENNILLE"

Network	ABC-TV
Airdates	September 20, 1976–March 14, 1977
Episodes	19

"THE STARLAND VOCAL BAND"

Network	CBS-TV
Airdates	July 31, 1977–September 2, 1977
Episodes	6

"THE MARILYN McCOO AND BILLY DAVIS JR. SHOW"

Network	ABC-TV
Airdates	June 15, 1977–July 20, 1977
Episodes	7

The Captain & Tennille had their own network series during the 1976–1977 TV season

"THE TONI TENNILLE SHOW"

Network   Syndicated

Airdates   September 1980–1981

"SHA NA NA"

Network   Syndicated

Airdates   September 1977–1981

Episodes   97

"THE WOLFMAN JACK SHOW"

Network   Syndicated

Airdates   October 1977–1978

Episodes   26

"PINK LADY" (ALSO KNOWN AS "PINK LADY AND JEFF")

Network	NBC-TV
Airdates	March 1, 1980–April 4, 1980
Episodes	6

"DOLLY" (HOSTED BY DOLLY PARTON)

Network	Syndicated
Airdates	September 1976–August 1978
Episodes	52

"DOLLY PARTON"

Network	ABC-TV
Airdates	September 27, 1987–1988

"THE NEW MONKEES"

Network	Syndicated
Airdates	September 1987–December 1987

Rock & Roll Dance Party TV Shows

"AMERICAN BANDSTAND"

Host/Producer	Dick Clark
Network	Various (see below)
Airdates	WFIL-TV Philadelphia/ September 1952–August 1957
	ABC-TV (nationally broadcast)/ August 5, 1957–September 5, 1987
	Syndicated (nationally)/ September 19, 1987–1990

"SHINDIG"

Host	Jimmy O'Neal
Network	ABC-TV
Airdates	September 16, 1964–January 5, 1966

"HULLABALOO!"

Host	Various
Network	NBC-TV
Airdates	January 12, 1965–August 29, 1966
Regular performers	The Hullabaloo Dancers

"WHERE THE ACTION IS"

Host/Producer	Dick Clark
Network	ABC-TV
Airdates	July 5, 1965–April 14, 1967
Regular guests	Paul Revere and the Raiders, Steve Alaimo, Linda Scott

"SOUL TRAIN"

Host/Producer	Don Cornelius
Network	Syndicated
Airdates	1970–present
Regular guests	The Soul Train Dancers

"TOP OF THE POPS"

Hosts	Various
Network	BBC (Great Britain)
Airdates	January 1, 1964–present

"DANCE PARTY U.S.A."

Host	Andy Gury
Network	USA Cable
Airdates	April 5, 1986–present

Rock Concert TV Series

"THE MIDNIGHT SPECIAL"

Announcers	Wolfman Jack and Mike Carruthers
Host	New one each week (1973–1975) / Helen Reddy (1975–1976)
Network	NBC-TV
Airdates	February 2, 1973–May 1, 1981

"DON KIRSHNER'S ROCK CONCERT"

Host/Producer	Don Kirshner
Network	Syndicated
Airdates	1973–1981

"IN CONCERT"

Host	New one each week
Network	ABC-TV
Airdates	January 1973–May 1975

"SOLID GOLD"

Hosts included	Dionne Warwick, Marilyn McCoo, Andy Gibb, Rex Smith, Rick Dees
Network	Syndicated
Airdates	September 1980–1988

Fine Artists as Album Cover Artists

PETER MAX

1995 Grammy Nominees (1995)

(I Got No Kick Against) Modern Jazz: A GRP Artists' Celebration of the Songs of the Beatles (1995)

Talk, Yes (1994)

Jerico, The Band (1993)

Through the Storm, Aretha Franklin (1989)

ANDY WARHOL

Aretha, Aretha Franklin (1986)

Silk Electric, Diana Ross (1982)

Emotions in Motion, Billy Squire (1982)

Sticky Fingers, The Rolling Stones (1971)

The Velvet Underground and Nico, The Velvet Underground and Nico (1967)

H. R. GIGER

Koo Koo, Debbie Harry (1981)

Brain Salad Surgery, Emerson, Lake & Palmer (1975)

Patti Smith as photographed by the controversial Robert Mapplethorpe for her 1988 *Dream of Life* album

ALBERTO VARGAS

Bernadette Peters, Bernadette Peters (1980)

Candy O, The Cars (1979)

ROBERT MAPPLETHORPE

Dream of Life, Patti Smith (1988)

Horses, Patti Smith (1975)

CAT STEVENS

Teaser and the Firecat, Cat Stevens (1971)

Tea for the Tillerman, Cat Stevens (1970)

Mona Bone Jakon, Cat Stevens (1970)

JONI MITCHELL

Turbulent Indigo, Joni Mitchell (1994)

Dog Eat Dog, Joni Mitchell (1985)

Wild Things Run Fast, Joni Mitchell (1982)

Mingus, Joni Mitchell (1979)

The Hissing of Summer Lawns, Joni Mitchell (1975)

So Far, Crosby, Stills, Nash & Young (1974)

Miles of Aisles, Joni Mitchell (1974)

Court and Spark, Joni Mitchell (1974)

Ladies of the Canyon, Joni Mitchell (1970)

Clouds, Joni Mitchell (1969)

Joni Mitchell, Joni Mitchell (1968)

LEROY NIEMAN

Portrait, The Fifth Dimension (1970)

GEORGE HURRELL

Press to Play, Paul and Linda McCartney (1986)

Love All the Hurt Away, Aretha Franklin (1981)

Rock Songs About the Phone

The Village People in 1988: *(Left to right)* Randy Jones, Felipe Rose, Alex Briley, Ray Simpson, David Hodo, Glenn Hughes

"Call Me"	Chris Montez (1966)
"Beechwood 4-5789"	The Marvelettes (1962); The Carpenters (1982)
"Sex Over the Phone"	Village People (1985)
"634-5789"	Wilson Pickett (1966)
"Call Me"	Aretha Franklin (1970)
"Telephone Line"	Electric Light Orchestra (1977)
"Call Me (Come Back Home)"	Al Green (1973)
"Ring My Phone"	Tommy Sands (1957)

"Operator"	The Manhattan Transfer (1975)
"Operator"	The Grateful Dead (1970)
"Operator (That's Not the Way It Feels)"	Jim Croce (1972)
"Memphis"	Johnny Rivers (1964); Chuck Berry (1958)
"Hanging on the Telephone"	Blondie (1978)
"867-5309/Jenny"	Tommy Tutone (1982)

Rock Songs About Cars

Gladys Knight & the Pips: *(Left to right)* Merald "Bubba" Knight, Edward Pattan, William Guest

"GTO"	Ronnie & the Datonas (1964)
"409"	The Beach Boys (1962)
"Drive My Car"	The Beatles (1965)
"Fast Car"	Tracy Chapman (1988)
"Pink Cadillac"	Natalie Cole (1988)
"Freeway of Love"	Aretha Franklin (1985)
"Expressway to Your Heart"	The Soul Survivors (1967)

"Car Wash"	Rose Royce (1977)
"Drivin' Wheel"	Foghat (1977)
"The End of the Road"	Gladys Knight & the Pips (1968)
"Motoring"	Martha Reeves & the Vandellas (1965)
"You're My Driving Wheel"	The Supremes (1976)
"I Can't Drive 55"	Sammy Hagar (1984)
"Drive"	The Cars (1984)
"Cars"	Gary Numan (1980)
"Steamy Windows"	Tina Turner (1989)
"Mercedes Benz"	Janis Joplin (1971)

Rock Stars Named After Colors

Jackson Browne

- Simply Red
- Red Hot Chili Peppers
- Red Rider
- Otis Redding
- King Crimson
- Rose Royce
- Pink Floyd
- Pink Lady
- New Riders of the Purple Sage
- Deep Purple
- The Moody Blues
- The Blues Magoos
- The Bluejays
- The Blues Brothers
- Blue Oyster Cult
- Blue Cheer
- Blues Image
- Blues Project
- Blues Traveler
- Shocking Blue
- Bobby "Blue" Bland
- Harold Melvin & the Blue Notes
- Al Green
- Peter Green
- Green Day
- Norman Greenbaum
- Greenslade
- Jimmy Greenspoon
  (Three Dog Night)

- Arthur Brown
- Bobby Brown
- James Brown
- Peter Brown
- Roy Brown
- Ruth Brown
- Jackson Browne
- Brownstone
- Brownsville Station
- Barry White
- Whitesnake
- Black Crows
- Black Kangaroo
- Black Oak Arkansas
- Black Sabbath
- Cilla Black
- Jay Black & the Americans
- Joan Jett and the Blackhearts
- Silver Convention
- Quicksilver Messenger Service
- Golden Earring
- Andrew Gold
- Yellow Magic Orchestra
- Yellow Balloon
- Ritchie Blackmore's Rainbow
- Living Colour

Rock Stars with Numbered Names

The B-52's circa 1980: *(Left to right)* Fred Schneider, Cindy Wilson, Ricky Wilson, Keith Strickland, Kate Pierson

- The Fifth Dimension
- We Five
- 10cc
- The Jackson Five
- U2
- 10,000 Maniacs
- The B-52's
- Take Six
- L7
- The MC5
- All-4-One
- Count Five
- The Third Rail

- 4 Non-Blondes
- Nine Inch Nails
- Heaven 17
- Ten Years After
- Ten Wheel Drive
- The Four Tops
- The Four Seasons
- Haircut 100
- .38 Special
- UB40
- Jive Five
- The Thirteenth Floor Elevators
- The First Edition

Rock Groups Named After Fruit (and the Songs That Made Them Famous)

Eric Carmen of The Raspberries

The Strawberry Alarm Clock	"Incense and Peppermints" (1967)
The Lemon Pipers	"Green Tambourine" (1968)
Wild Cherry	"Play That Funky Music" (1976)
Neneh Cherry	"Buffalo Stance" (1988)
The Electric Prunes	"I Had Too Much to Dream (Last Night)" (1967)
Moby Grape	"Omaha" (1967)
Bananarama	"Cruel Summer" (1984)
The Limelighters	"A Dollar Down" (1961)
The Raspberries	"Go All the Way" (1972)
The Applejacks	"Mexican Hat Rock" (1958)
The Cranberries	"Zombie" (1994)
Blind Melon	"No Rain" (1993)
Grapefruit	"Dear Delilah" (1968)
The Lemonheads	"Into Your Arms" (1993)
Smashing Pumpkins	"Disarm" (1993)

Rock Stars with Geographic Names

- Boston
- Chicago
- America
- Europe
- Asia
- Hiroshima
- The Manhattan Transfer
- The Atlanta Rhythm Section
- The Detroit Emeralds
- Buffalo Springfield
- The Ohio Players
- The L.A. Jets
- John Denver
- The Bay City Rollers
- The Georgia Satellites
- Kansas
- STYX
- Mitch Ryder & the Detroit Wheels
- Alabama
- TSOP (The Sound of Philadelphia)
- Art in America

America: *(Left to right)* Dewey Bunnell, Gerry Beckley, Dan Peek

- Black Oak Arkansas
- The New York Dolls
- Marcella Detroit
- Thelma Houston
- Whitney Houston
- Cissy Houston
- Julie London
- Berlin
- Herb Alpert & the Tijuana Brass
- The Miami Sound Machine
- Country Dick Montana (Beat Farmers)
- Handsome Dick Manitoba (The Dictators)
- Jello Biafra
- Ozark Mountain Daredevils
- Brownsville Station
- Texas Tornadoes
- Illinois Speed Press
- Frankie Goes to Hollywood
- The Manhattans

Rock Stars' Former Occupations

MARY WILSON (THE SUPREMES)

clerk in a record shop

KEITH MOON (THE WHO)

plaster salesperson

ELVIS PRESLEY

truck driver

MARTHA REEVES

clerk at a dry cleaners

DEBBIE HARRY

Playboy bunny

Pat Benatar

PAT BENATAR

bank teller

JON BON JOVI

Burger King employee

MADONNA

hat-check girl

clerk at Dunkin' Donuts

nude model for art students

DAVID BOWIE

art teacher

ANNIE LENNOX (EURYTHMICS)

fish filleter in a factory

Eurythmics: Dave Stewart and Annie Lennox

TERENCE TRENT D'ARBY

corporal in the army

LOU REED

accountant's assistant

PETER GABRIEL (GENESIS)

travel agent

MICK JAGGER
(THE ROLLING STONES)

ice-cream vendor

KEITH RICHARDS
(THE ROLLING STONES)

tennis-court ball boy

STING (THE POLICE)

schoolteacher

DARYL HALL (HALL & OATES)

apple picker

BOB GELDOF
(THE BOOMTOWN RATS)

pea sheller in a factory

SIMON LEBON (DURAN DURAN)

lumberjack

BELINDA CARLISLE
(THE GO-GO'S)

gas-station attendant

DR. JOHN

child model (was an Ivory Snow baby)

ELVIS COSTELLO

computer programmer

CYNDI LAUPER

racehorse walker

ROD STEWART

grave digger

STEVIE NICKS
(FLEETWOOD MAC)

hostess at Bob's Big Boy restaurant

PETER WOLF
(THE J. GEILS BAND)

radio disk jockey

ROGER DALTRY (THE WHO)

sheet-metal worker

MICKY DOLENZ (THE MONKEES)

child star of TV show "Circus Boy"

M.C. HAMMER

bat boy for the Oakland A's

GEORGE MICHAEL

movie-theater usher

CHRIS ISAAK

tour guide in Japan

JON KNIGHT
(NEW KIDS ON THE BLOCK)

Burger King employee

BETTE MIDLER

pineapple-packing plant worker

go-go dancer

DAVY JONES (THE MONKEES)

child star in Broadway's *Oliver*

VINCE NEIL (MÖTLEY CRÜE)

electrician

DONNIE WAHLBERG
(NEW KIDS ON THE BLOCK)

shoe salesman

LITTLE EVA

babysitter for Carole King's children

Rock Star Drug Overdoses

Tommy Bolin	December 4, 1976
John Bonham (Led Zeppelin)	September 25, 1980
Tim Buckley	June 29, 1975
Paul Butterfield	May 4, 1987
David Byron (Uriah Heep)	February 19, 1980
Brian Cole (The Association)	August 2, 1972
Pete Farndon (The Pretenders)	April 14, 1983
Tim Hardin	December 29, 1980
Jimi Hendrix	September 18, 1970
Bob Hite (Canned Heat)	April 6, 1981
James Honeyman-Scott (The Pretenders)	June 16, 1982
Shannon Hoon (Blind Melon)	October 21, 1995
Janis Joplin	October 4, 1970
Frankie Lyman (Frankie Lyman and the Teenagers)	February 28, 1968
Phil Lynott (Thin Lizzy)	January 4, 1986
Robbie McIntosh (Average White Band)	September 23, 1974
Keith Moon (The Who)	September 7, 1978
Billy Murcia (The New York Dolls)	November 6, 1972
Brent Mydland (The Grateful Dead)	July 26, 1990
Jon Jon Paulus (The Buckinghams)	March 26, 1980

David Ruffin (The Temptations)   June 1, 1991

Bon Scott (AC/DC)   February 19, 1980

Gary Thain (Uriah Heep)   March 19, 1976

Johnny Thunders (The New York Dolls)   April 23, 1991

Sid Vicious (Sex Pistols)   February 2, 1979

Danny Whitten (Buffalo Springfield)   November 18, 1972

Alan Wilson (Canned Heat)   September 3, 1970

The Who: *(Left to right)* Keith Moon, Pete Townshend, Roger Daltry, John Entwistle

Rock Stars Who Died Too Soon

The Carpenters: Richard and Karen

Duane Allman (Allman Brothers Band)	24	October 29, 1971	motorcycle accident
Florence Ballard (The Supremes)	32	February 22, 1976	heart failure
Big Bopper	28	February 3, 1959	plane crash
Marc Bolan (T. Rex)	30	September 17, 1977	car accident
Cliff Burton (Metallica)	24	September 27, 1986	tour bus accident
Karen Carpenter (The Carpenters)	32	February 4, 1983	cardiac arrest caused by anorexia nervosa
Eric Carr (KISS)	41	November 24, 1991	cancer
Harry Chapin	38	July 16, 1981	car accident
John Cipollina (Quicksilver Messenger Service)	45	May 29, 1989	liver failure
Gene Clark (The Byrds)	46	May 24, 1991	heart attack
Michael Clark (The Byrds)	50	December 19, 1993	liver failure
Patsy Cline	30	March 5, 1963	plane crash
Kurt Cobain (Nirvana)	27	April 8, 1994	suicide

Eddie Cochran	21	April 17, 1960	car accident
Allen Collins (Lynyrd Skynyrd)	age unknown	October 20, 1977	plane crash
Sam Cooke	29	December 10, 1964	murdered by gunshot
Jim Croce	30	September 20, 1973	plane crash
Bobby Darin	37	December 20, 1973	died during heart surgery
Sandy Denny (Fairport Convention)	31	April 21, 1978	brain hemorrhage
Mama Cass Elliot (The Mamas & the Papas)	33	July 29, 1974	heart attack induced by choking
Tom Evans (Badfinger)	36	November 18, 1983	suicide
Tom Fogerty (Creedence Clearwater Revival)	48	September 6, 1990	respiratory failure
Melvin Franklin (The Temptations)	52	February 23, 1995	heart failure
Bobby Fuller (The Bobby Fuller Four)	22	July 18, 1966	death by orally consuming gasoline (foul play suspected)

The Temptations in 1978: Melvin Franklin *(center)* with *(left to right)* Otis Williams, Glenn Leonard, Richard Street, and Lois Price

Billy Fury	41	January 28, 1983	heart attack
Cassie Gaines (background singer for Lynyrd Skynyrd)	age unknown	October 20, 1977	plane crash
Steven Gaines (Lynyrd Skynyrd)	age unknown	October 20, 1977	plane crash
Rory Gallagher	47	July 1995	pneumonia, following a liver transplant

Jerry Garcia (Grateful Dead)	53	August 9, 1995	heart attack at the Betty Ford Clinic, following years of heroin and other drug use
Marvin Gaye	44	April 1, 1984	murdered, by gunshot, by his father
Lowell George (Little Feat)	34	June 29, 1979	heart attack, following years of drug abuse
Andy Gibb	30	March 10, 1980	heart virus
John Glascock (Jethro Tull)	28	November 21, 1979	heart failure
Keith Godchaux (The Grateful Dead)	31	July 23, 1980	motorcycle accident
Rick Grech (Blind Faith)	44	March 17, 1990	effects of long-term drug abuse
Martin Hale (Spanky and Our Gang)	27	1968	cirrhosis of the liver
Pete Ham (Badfinger)	27	April 23, 1975	suicide
Adie "Micki" Harris (The Shirelles)	42	June 10, 1982	heart attack
Donny Hathaway	33	January 13, 1979	suicide

Buddy Holly	22	February 3, 1959	plane crash
Phyllis Hyman	45	June 30, 1995	apparently pill-induced suicide
O'Kelly Isley (The Isley Brothers)	48	March 31, 1986	heart attack
Brian Jones (The Rolling Stones)	27	July 3, 1969	drowned
Terry Kath (Chicago)	31	January 23, 1978	suicide
Eddie Kendricks (The Temptations)	52	October 5, 1992	lung cancer
Paul Kossoff (Free)	25	March 19, 1976	heart failure on a transatlantic jet, following years of drug abuse
John Lennon (The Beatles)	40	December 8, 1980	murdered
Richard Manuel (The Band)	42	March 4, 1986	suicide
Steve Marriott (Humble Pie)	44	April 20, 1991	death due to fire in his house
Jimmy McCullouch (Thunderclap Newman/Wings)	26	September 27, 1979	heart failure

Ron McKernan (Pigpen) (The Grateful Dead)	27	March 8, 1973	liver disease
Freddie Mercury (Queen)	45	November 24, 1991	AIDS
Country Dick Montana (The Beat Farmers)	40	November 8, 1995	aneurysm, collapsed on stage
Jim Morrison (The Doors)	27	July 3, 1971	heart attack in a Paris bathtub, induced by respiratory problems
Ricky Nelson	45	December 31, 1985	plane crash
Harry Nilsson	52	January 15, 1994	heart attack
Berry Oakley (Allman Brothers Band)	24	November 11, 1972	motorcycle accident
Phil Ochs	35	April 9, 1976	suicide
Roy Orbison	52	December 6, 1988	heart attack
Felix Papalardi (Mountain)	44	April 17, 1983	murdered, by gunshot, by his wife, Gail
Gram Parsons (The Byrds, The Flying Burrito Brothers)	26	July 14, 1973	heart failure

Jeff Porcaro (Toto)	38	August 5, 1992	mysterious chemical reaction suspected; was spraying garden insecticide with cocaine in his bloodstream
Dave Prather (Sam and Dave)	50	April 9, 1988	car accident
Elvis Presley	42	August 16, 1977	cardiac arrest
Danny Rapp (Danny & the Juniors)	41	April 8, 1983	suicide
Otis Redding	26	December 10, 1967	plane crash
Keith Relf (The Yardbirds)	33	May 14, 1976	accidental electrocution
Minnie Ripperton	31	July 12, 1979	cancer
Del Shannon	50	February 8, 1990	suicide
Stu Sutcliff (The Silver Beetles)	22	April 10, 1962	brain hemorrhage
Tammi Terrell	24	March 16, 1970	brain tumor
Steve Peregrine-Took (T. Rex)	age unknown	October 27, 1980	choking
Ritchie Valens	17	February 3, 1959	plane crash

Ronnie Van Zant (Lynyrd Skynyrd)	28	October 20, 1977	plane crash
Stevie Ray Vaughan	35	August 27, 1990	helicopter crash
Junior Walker	53	November 23, 1995	cancer
Mary Wells	49	July 26, 1992	cancer
Clarence White (The Byrds)	29	July 14, 1973	struck by an automobile
Ronnie White (The Miracles)	56	August 26, 1995	leukemia
Dennis Wilson (The Beach Boys)	39	December 28, 1983	drowned
Jackie Wilson	49	January 21, 1984	heart attack following an eight-year coma
Ricky Wilson (The B-52's)	32	October 12, 1985	AIDS
Wolfman Jack (rock DJ)	57	July 1, 1995	heart attack
Chris Wood (Traffic)	39	July 12, 1983	liver failure
Frank Zappa (The Mothers of Invention)	52	December 4, 1993	prostate cancer

Rock Stars Who Drowned in Their Own Vomit

JIMI HENDRIX

On the night of September 18, 1970, Jimi took a handful of Vesperax sleeping pills, smoked pot, and drank white wine. He fell asleep on his back, vomited, and drowned in his own vomit.

MAMA CASS ELLIOT

When Mama Cass died on July 29, 1974, she was eating a sandwich. She began vomiting up part of the sandwich she had just eaten, inhaled the vomit, and, beginning to asphyxiate, had a heart attack. As the sad joke goes, "If Mama Cass had simply shared her sandwich with Karen Carpenter, they might both be alive today!"

Rock Stars Who Have Publicly Admitted to Being Bisexual, Gay, or Lesbian

The Indigo Girls (Emily Saliers *[left]*, Amy Ray *[right]*) with Melissa Etheridge (*center*) at the Roxy in L.A. in 1989

Amy Ray (Indigo Girls)
Emily Saliers (Indigo Girls)
Elton John
David Bowie (bi)
k.d. lang
Melissa Etheridge
Holly Johnson (Frankie Goes to Hollywood)
Madonna (bi)

Boy George
Michael Stipe (R.E.M.)
Jimmy Somerville (Bronski Beat)
Joan Baez (bi)
Janis Ian
Pete Townshend (bi)
Paul Rutherford (Frankie Goes to Hollywood)

Male Rock Stars Who Have Worn the Most Excessive Amounts of Facial Makeup in Public

KISS in full makeup in the 1970s

Michael Jackson

Little Richard

Prince

KISS

David Bowie

Mick Jagger

RuPaul

Adam Ant

Elvis Presley

The New York Dolls

Dead or Alive

Pete Burns of the group Dead or Alive

Boy George

Gary Numan

Philip Oakey (Human League)

Gary Glitter

Best Cross-Dressing Displays by Rock Stars

David Bowie in his flamboyant period, promoting his 1980 album *Scary Monsters*

Elton John as Tina Turner/Madison Square Garden (1986)

Annie Lennox as Elvis Presley/The Grammy Awards (1985)

David Bowie in his "Fashion" video (1980)

Mick Jagger in the film *Performance* (1970)

RuPaul in his "Supermodel" video (1993)

Tim Curry as Dr. Frankenfurter in the movie *The Rocky Horror Picture Show* (1975)

The 10 Juiciest Rock & Roll Scandals

Elvis Presley's Death (1977)

Following years of prescription-drug abuse and overeating, the King of Rock & Roll died sad and bloated in his bathroom.

Michael Jackson's Sex Scandal (1993–1994)

After a decade of declaring his love of children, the self-proclaimed Prince of Pop was accused of sexually abusing young boys. The problem was solved by a multimillion-dollar payment to the accusing child and the boy's parents.

Madonna caused a commotion with her 1992 book, *Sex*

MICHAEL JACKSON
MARRYING LISA MARIE PRESLEY
(1994)

Embroiled in the sex scandal, Jackson and Lisa Marie exchanged vows on May 26. Critics were so skeptical that the couple went on national television in June of 1995 to publicly proclaim that they sleep in the same bed.

MADONNA'S SEX BOOK
(1992)

Posing in various states of undress, and in sexually compromising positions with men, women, and animals, the "Like a Virgin" star was branded a "slut," but the book promptly hit Number One.

JERRY LEE LEWIS MARRYING HIS 13-YEAR-OLD COUSIN, MYRA, WHEN HE WAS 22 (1958)

By some standards, the idea of a 13-year-old bride may not seem so shocking, but by marrying cousin Myra Gale Brown, Jerry Lee ruined his red-hot career. He was shunned by the public for several years.

ANGELA BOWIE DISCOVERING HER HUSBAND, DAVID, IN BED WITH MICK JAGGER (MID-'70S)

Angela dropped this bombshell on "The Joan Rivers Show" in the early '90s, and promptly got a publication deal for her book *Backstage Passes*.

JOHN PHILLIPS DOING COKE WITH HIS DAUGHTER, MACKENZIE (1970S AND 1980S)

The leader of the Mamas & the Papas and his TV star daughter proved "the family that plays together stays together" by checking into a rehab clinic together in 1981.

MARVIN GAYE MURDERED BY HIS OWN FATHER (1984)

Marvin Gaye's father shot the singing legend after a domestic argument in the family's home.

JOHN LENNON'S ASSASSINATION (1980)

At the hands of a crazed fan, the former Beatle was gunned down in the entranceway of his apartment building, the Dakota, in New York City, while his wife, Yoko Ono, looked on in helpless horror.

THE MILLI VANILLI SCAM (1990)

After winning a Best New Artist Grammy Award, the duo known as Milli Vanilli admitted that they hadn't sung a single note on their platinum album. The award was promptly rescinded.

Rockers' Automobiles

Daryl Hall & John Oates in 1975

Micky Dolenz (The Monkees)	VW minibus
Mary Wilson (The Supremes)	Rolls-Royce
Jimmy Greenspoon (Three Dog Night)	Camaro
Bono (U2)	Mercedes-Benz
Daryl Hall (Hall & Oates)	Jeep

David Bowie	Volvo
Roland Gift (Fine Young Cannibals)	SAAB
John Lennon	Rolls-Royce
Martha Reeves	Buick Electra 225
Elvis Presley	Cadillac, Mercedes-Benz
Debbie Gibson	Thunderbird
M. C. Hammer	Porsche
Mick Fleetwood	Jeep
Janet Jackson	Mercedes-Benz
Mick Jagger	Ferrari
Elton John	Bentley
Madonna	Mercedes-Benz, Thunderbird
Michael McDonald (The Doobie Brothers)	Chevy truck
Mike Mills (R.E.M.)	Thunderbird
Mark Bego (rock author)	Cadillac Eldorado
Paula Abdul	Jaguar
Paul McCartney	Mercedes-Benz

Rock Stars'
Autobiographies

Debbie Gibson

Martha Reeves
> *Dancing in the Street: Confessions of a Motown Diva*

Debbie Gibson
> *Between the Lines*

Mary Wilson
> *Dreamgirl: My Life as a Supreme*
> *Supreme Faith: Someday We'll Be Together*

Micky Dolenz
I'm a Believer: My Life of Music, Monkees, and Madness

Jimmy Greenspoon (Three Dog Night)
One Is the Loneliest Number

John Phillips (The Mamas & the Papas)
Papa John

Michelle Phillips (The Mamas & the Papas)
California Dreamin'

David Crosby
Long Time Gone

Otis Williams
Temptations

LaToya Jackson
Growing Up in the Jackson Family

Angela Bowie
Backstage Passes

Judy Collins
Trust Your Heart

Bob Geldof
Is That It?

Smokey Robinson
Inside Myself

Brian Wilson (The Beach Boys)
Wouldn't It Be Nice

Mick Fleetwood
My Life and Adventures in Fleetwood Mac

David Cassidy (The Partridge Family)
C'mon Get Happy

Holly Near
Fire in the Rain . . . Singer in the Storm

Priscilla Presley
Elvis and Me

Ronnie Spector
Be My Baby

Sonny Bono
And the Beat Goes On

Connie Francis

Diana Ross
>   *Secrets of a Sparrow*

Joan Baez
>   *And a Voice to Sing With*

Connie Francis
>   *Who's Sorry Now?*

Marianne Faithful
>   *Faithful*

Wolfman Jack
>   *Have Mercy: The Confession of the Original Party Animal*

Berry Gordy Jr.
>   *To Be Loved*

Rock Stars with One Name

The Police: *(Left to right)* Andy Summers, Stuart Copeland, and Sting

Cher	Meatloaf
Melanie	Fish (Marillion)
Madonna	Twiggy
Lulu	Donovan
Sting	Björk
Bono (U2)	Snow
Prince	Junior
Dion	

Rockers with Animal Names

Rock & roll cat: Cat Stevens

The Beatles

Three Dog Night

The Animals

The Turtles

Sheryl Crow

Snoop Doggy Dogg

Iron Butterfly

The Monkees

Echo & the Bunnymen

Hootie & the Blowfish

The Flamingos

The Butterflies

Adam & the Ants

Zebra

Buddy Holly & the Crickets

The Byrds

Country Joe & the Fish

Buffalo Springfield

The Murmaids

The Eagles

Cat Stevens

Stray Cats

Toad the Wet Sprocket

The Fabulous Poodles

Bunny Wailer

Black Kangaroo

Inez & Charlie Foxx

Hot Tuna

Rhinoceros

Crazy Horse

Dinosaur Jr.

The Chipmunks

Flock of Seagulls

Fabulous Thunderbirds

Los Lobos

The Polecats

The Penguins

Elephant's Memory

Rock & roll dogs: Three Dog Night

Rock Stars' Real Names

Adam Ant	Stuart Goddard
Frankie Avalon	Francis Avallone
Pat Benatar	Patricia Andrzejewski
Brook Benton	Benjamin Franklin Peak
Kurtis Blow	Kurt Walker
Sonny Bono	Salvatore Bono
Big Bopper	J. P. Richardson
David Bowie	David Robert Jones
Freddie Cannon	Frederick Anthony Picariello
Captain Beefheart	Don Van Vliet
Ray Charles	Ray Charles Robinson
Chubby Checker	Ernest Evans
Cher	Cherilyn Sarkasian LaPier
Lou Christie	Lugee Geno Saco
Jimmy Cliff	James Chambers
Patsy Cline	Virginia Patterson Hensley
Bootsy Collins	William Collins
Commander Cody	George Frayne Boise
Alice Cooper	Vincent Furnier
Elvis Costello	Declan McManus
Bobby Darin	Walden Robert Cassotto
Joey Dee	Joseph Dinicola
John Denver	John Henry Deutschendorf
Rick Derringer	Rick Zehringer
Bo Diddley	Elias Bates
Dion	Dion DiMucci
Neil Diamond	Noah Kaminsky
Dr. John	Malcom "Mac" Rebennack
Fats Domino	Antoine Domino
Donovan	Donovan Leitch

Lonnie Donegan	Anthony Donegan
Bob Dylan	Robert Allen Zimmerman
Brian Eno	Brian Peter George St. John de Baptiste de la Salle Eno
David Essex	David Cook
Fabian	Fabian Forte
Georgie Fame	Clive Powell
Freddy Fender	Baldemar Huerta
Connie Francis	Concetta Franconero
Billy Fury	Ronald Wycherly
Bobbie Gentry	Bobbie Lee Street
Gary Glitter	Paul Francis Gadd
Screamin' Jay Hawkins	Jalacy Hawkins
Buddy Holly	Charles Hardin Holley
Cissy Houston	Emily Drinkard
Janis Ian	Janis Eddy Fink
Billy Idol	Willem Wolfe Broad
Rick James	James Johnson
Little Willie John	William J. Woods
Elton John	Dwight Kenneth Dwight
Chaka Khan	Yvette Marie Stevens
B.B. King	Riley B. King
Ben E. King	Benjamin Earl Soloman
Carole King	Carole Klein
Patti LaBelle	Patricia Louise Holt
Brenda Lee	Brenda Mae Tarpley
Little Anthony	Anthony Gourdine
Little Eva	Eva Narcissus Boyd
Little Richard	Richard Penniman
Darlene Love	Darlene Wright
Lulu	Marie McDonald Mclaughlin Lawrie
Melanie	Melanie Safka
Joni Mitchell	Roberta Joan Anderson
Eddie Money	Edward Mahoney
Country Dick Montana	Daniel McLain
Maria Muldaur	Maria Grazia Rosa Domenica d'Amato
Van Morrison	George Ivan
Ricky Nelson	Eric Hilliard Nelson
Harry Nilsson	Harry Edward Nelson III
Tony Orlando	Michael Anthony Orlando Cassavitis

Gilbert O'Sullivan	Raymond O'Sullivan
Gram Parsons	Cecil Connor
Les Paul	Lester Polfus
Prince	Prince Rogers Nelson
P.J. Proby	James Marcus Smith
Genya Ravan	Goldie Zelkowitz
Johnny Rotten	John Lydon
Leon Russell	Hank Wilson
Mitch Ryder	William Levise Jr.
Boz Scaggs	William Royce Scaggs
Seal	Sealhenry Samuel
Del Shannon	Charles Westover
Phoebe Snow	Phoebe Laub
Spanky McFarlane	Elaine McFarlane
Ronnie Spector	Veronica Bennett
Dusty Springfield	Mary O'Brien
Edwin Starr	Charles Hatcher
Cat Stevens	Steven Georgiou
Donna Summer	Donna Gaines
Sly Stone	Sylvester Stewart
Ringo Starr	Richard Starkey
Sting	Gordon Sumner
Tina Turner	Annie Mae Bullock
Bobby Vee	Robert Velline
Gene Vincent	Eugene Vincent Craddock
Junior Walker	Autry DeWalt Walker Jr.
Don Was	Donald Fagenson
Stevie Wonder	Steveland Morris

Rockers Who Went Disco

CHER

"Take Me Home" (1979)

THE ROLLING STONES

"Miss You" (1978)

CAROLE KING

"Hard Rock Cafe" (1977)

ARETHA FRANKLIN

"Jump to It" (1982)

THE SUPREMES

"I'm Gonna Let My Heart Do the Walking" (1976)

"You're My Driving Wheel" (1977)

Rod Stewart

ROD STEWART

"Da Ya Think I'm Sexy?" (1979)

MARY WILSON

"Red Hot" (1979)

BLONDIE

"Heart of Glass" (1979)

"Call Me" (1980)

MARTHA REEVES

"Skating in the Streets" (1980)

Blondie

THE BEE GEES

"Stayin' Alive" (1978)

DIANA ROSS

"Love Hangover" (1976)

"I'm Coming Out" (1980)

"Upside Down" (1980)

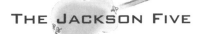

THE JACKSON FIVE

"Dancing Machine" (1974)

PEACHES AND HERB

"Shake Your Groove Thing" (1978)

BETTE MIDLER

"Strangers in the Night" (1976)
"My Knight in Black Leather" (1979)
"Married Men" (1979)

RINGO STARR

"Drowning in the Sea of Love" (1977)

CARLY SIMON

"Why" (1982)

Rock Stars Who Released Jazz Albums

LINDA RONSTADT

JAZZ ALBUMS

- *What's New* (Elektra Records/1983)
- *Lush Life* (Elektra Records/1986)
- *For Sentimental Reasons* (Elektra Records/1986)

CD PACKAGE

- *'Round Midnight* (Elektra Records/1986) [Boxed set of all of the above three albums, produced by Nelson Riddle himself]

TONI TENNILLE (THE CAPTAIN AND TENNILLE)

JAZZ ALBUMS

- *More Than You Know* (Atlantic Records/1984)
- *All of Me* (Gaia Records/1987)

Carly Simon

CARLY SIMON

JAZZ ALBUMS

- *Torch* (Warner Brothers Records/1981)
- *My Romance* (Arista Records/1990)

DIONNE WARWICK

JAZZ ALBUM

- *Dionne Warwick Sings Cole Porter* (Arista Records/1990)

ARETHA FRANKLIN

JAZZ ALBUMS

- *Unforgettable—A Tribute to Dinah Washington* (Columbia Records/1964)
- *Yeah!!!* (Columbia Records/1965)
- *Sweet Bitter Love* (Columbia Records/1982)
- *Aretha's Jazz* (Atlantic Records/1984)
- *After Hours* (Columbia Records/1987)

CD PACKAGES

- *Aretha Sings the Blues* (Columbia Records/1985)
- *Jazz to Soul* (Columbia Records/1992)

THE SUPREMES

JAZZ ALBUM

- *The Supremes Sing Rodgers and Hart* (Motown Records/1967)

CD PACKAGE

- *The Rodgers & Hart Collection* (Motown Records/1987) [Extended CD version of 1967 album, with 12 extra cuts]

BARRY MANILOW

JAZZ ALBUMS

- *Swing Street* (Arista Records/1987)
- *Singin' with the Big Bands* (Arista Records/1994)

CHAKA KHAN

JAZZ ALBUM

- *Echoes of an Era* (Elektra Records/1982) [This masterpiece of jazz singing is an ensemble jazz group, with Chaka singing alongside star musicians Chick Corea, Stanley Clarke, Lenny White, Joe Henderson, and Freddie Hubbard]

SADE

JAZZ ALBUMS

- *Diamond Life* (Epic Records/1984) [Although all of Sade's albums are a synthesis of jazz and rock elements, this one is the jazziest classic of them all]
- *Promise* (Epic Records/1985)
- *Stronger Than Pride* (Epic Records/1988)
- *Love Deluxe* (Epic Records/1992)

MARVIN GAYE

JAZZ ALBUMS

- *Hello Broadway* (Motown Records/1964)
- *A Tribute to Nat King Cole* (Motown Records/1965)

Sade

NATALIE COLE

JAZZ ALBUMS

- *Unforgettable* (Elektra Records/1991)
- *Take a Look* (Elektra Records/1993)

THE MANHATTAN TRANSFER

JAZZ ALBUM

- *Vocalese* (Atlantic Records/1985) [Like Sade, it is hard to draw the line between jazz and rock on all of Manhattan Transfer's albums, but this one, written by Jon Hendricks of the legendary 1950s jazz vocal group Lambert, Hendricks, and Ross, is 100 percent jazz, and is brilliant]

CHER

JAZZ ALBUM

- *Bittersweet White Light* (MCA Records/1973)

SINÉAD O'CONNOR

JAZZ ALBUM

- *Am I Not Your Girl?* (Ensign Records/1992)

Rock Songs About Disaster

"Eve of Destruction"
  Barry McGuire (1965)
  The Turtles (1970)

"Deadman's Curve"
  Jan & Dean (1964)

"New York Mining Disaster 1941
(Have You Seen My Wife, Mr. Jones?)"
  The Bee Gees (1967)

The Bee Gees: *(Left to right)* Robin Gibb, Barry Gibb, Maurice Gibb

"Wipeout"
   The Safaris (1963/1966)

"Quicksand"
   Martha Reeves & the Vandellas (1964)

"Air Disaster"
   Albert Hammond (1974)

"War"
   Edwin Starr (1970)

"Waterloo"
   ABBA (1974)

"End of the World"
   Skeeter Davis (1963)

"Disco Inferno"
   The Trammps (1977)

Rock Songs About Monsters

"The Monster Mash"
   Bobby "Boris" Pickett (1962)

"Purple People Eater"
   Sheb Wooley (1958)

"The Eggplant That Ate Chicago"
   Dr. West's Medicine Show and Junk Band (1966)

"Purple People Eater Meets the Witch Doctor"
   Joe South (1958)

"Monster's Holiday"
   Bobby "Boris" Pickett (1962)

"Monster"
   Steppenwolf (1970)

"Frankenstein"
   The Edgar Winter Group (1973)

"Clap for the Wolfman"
   The Guess Who (1974)

"Werewolves of London"
   Warren Zevon (1978)

Psychedelic Soundtrack for the Summer of Love: 1967

"The Beat Goes On"
Sonny and Cher
Release date: January 1967

"Epistle to Dippy"
Donovan
Release date: January 1967

"For What It's Worth"
Buffalo Springfield
Release date: January 1967

"The 59th Street Bridge Song (Feelin' Groovy)"
Harpers Bizarre
Release date: January 1967

"California Nights"
Leslie Gore
Release date: February 1967

Art Garfunkel and Paul Simon in Central Park, 1981

"Strawberry Fields Forever"
  The Beatles
  Release date: February 1967

"Ruby Tuesday"
  The Rolling Stones
  Release date: February 1967

"At the Zoo"
  Simon & Garfunkel
  Release date: March 1967

"Creeque Alley"
  The Mamas and the Papas
  Release date: April 1967

"Groovin' "
  The Young Rascals
  Release date: April 1967

"The Happening"
The Supremes
Release date: April 1967

"Let's Live for Today"
The Grass Roots
Release date: April 1967

"Mirage"
Tommy James and the Shondells
Release date: April 1967

"My Back Pages"
The Byrds
Release date: April 1967

"Ain't No Mountain High Enough"
Marvin Gaye & Tammi Terrell
Release date: May 1967

"San Francisco (Be Sure to Wear Some Flowers in Your Hair)"
Scott McKenzie
Release date: May 1967

"Up, Up, and Away"
The Fifth Dimension
Release date: May 1967

"Windy"
The Association
Release date: May 1967

Sgt. Pepper's Lonely Hearts Club Band
The Beatles album (all cuts)
Release date: June 1967

"White Rabbit"
Jefferson Airplane
Release date: June 1967

"A Whiter Shade of Pale"
Procol Harum
Release date: June 1967

"Apples, Peaches, Pumpkin Pie"
Jay and the Techniques
Release date: July 1967

"Ode to Billie Joe"
Bobbie Gentry
Release date: July 1967

"Pleasant Valley Sunday"
The Monkees
Release date: July 1967

"Reflections"
The Supremes
Release date: July 1967

"San Franciscan Nights"
Eric Burdon and the Animals
Release date: July 1967

"Get Together"
The Youngbloods
Release date: August 1967

"Love Bug Leave My Heart Alone"
Martha and the Vandellas
Release date: August 1967

"Twelve Thirty (Young Girls Are Coming to the Canyon)"
The Mamas & the Papas
Release date: August 1967

"Incense and Peppermints"
The Strawberry Alarm Clock
Release date: September 1967

"King Midas in Reverse"
The Hollies
Release date: September 1967

"Lazy Day"
Spanky and Our Gang
Release date: September 1967

"The Rain, the Park and Other Things"
The Cowsills
Release date: September 1967

Are You Experienced?
The Jimi Hendrix album (all cuts)
Release date: September 1967

Fourteen of the Most Important Acts in Rock History

THE BEATLES

GROUP MEMBERS

John Lennon, Paul McCartney, George Harrison, Ringo Starr

NUMBER ONE HITS

- "I Want to Hold Your Hand" (1964)
- "She Loves You" (1964)
- "Can't Buy Me Love" (1964)
- "Love Me Do" (1964)
- "A Hard Day's Night" (1964)
- "I Feel Fine" (1964)
- "Eight Days a Week" (1965)
- "Ticket to Ride" (1965)

The Beatles: *(Clockwise from top)* George Harrison, John Lennon, Paul McCartney, and Ringo Starr

- "Help!" (1965)
- "Yesterday" (1965)
- "We Can Work It Out" (1965)
- "Paperback Writer" (1966)
- "Penny Lane" (1967)
- "All You Need Is Love" (1967)
- "Hello Goodbye" (1967)
- "Hey Jude" (1968)

- "Get Back" (1969)
- "Come Together" (1969)
- "Let It Be" (1970)
- "The Long and Winding Road" (1970)

MILESTONE ALBUMS (AMERICAN ALBUMS, WHICH DIFFER FROM THE BRITISH RELEASES AND SUBSEQUENT U.S. CDs)

- *Meet the Beatles* (1964)
- *The Beatles' Second Album* (1964)
- *A Hard Day's Night* (1964)
- *Something New* (1964)
- *Beatles' 65* (1965)
- *Beatles VI* (1965)
- *Help!* (1965)
- *Rubber Soul* (1965)
- *Yesterday . . . and Today* (1966)
- *Revolver* (1966)
- *Sgt. Pepper's Lonely Hearts Club Band* (1967)
- *Magical Mystery Tour* (1967)
- *The Beatles* [White Album] (1968)
- *Yellow Submarine* (1969)
- *Abbey Road* (1969)
- *Hey Jude* (1970)
- *Let It Be* (1970)
- *Rock 'n' Roll Music* [compilation] (1976)
- *The Beatles at the Hollywood Bowl* [1964 and 1965 performances] (1977)

NOTABLE CD PACKAGES

- *The Beatles 1962–1966* [Red Album] [2 CDs] (1973)
- *The Beatles 1967–1970* [Blue Album] [2 CDs] (1973)
- *The Beatles Live at the BBC* [2 CDs] (1994)
- *The Beatles Anthology 1* [2 CDs] (1995)

BEST JOHN LENNON SOLO ALBUM

- *Imagine* (1971)

BEST RINGO STARR SOLO ALBUM

- *Ringo* (1973)

BEST GEORGE HARRISON SOLO ALBUM

- *All Things Must Pass* (1970)

BEST PAUL McCARTNEY SOLO ALBUM

- *Band on the Run* [with Wings] (1973)

BAND HISTORY

Paul McCartney met John Lennon at a church picnic in their mutual hometown of Liverpool, England, on July 6, 1957. They became fast friends and made a pact that they would become a songwriting team. Little did they realize that they were destined to become the greatest songwriting duo in rock history. The pair joined an existing local group called The Quarrymen and met and befriended George Harrison. By November of the next year, the trio of Lennon/McCartney/Harrison formed their own group, called Johnny and the Moondogs. Then, with additional players Stu Sutcliffe on bass and Pete Best on drums, they performed as The Silver Beetles for a time. On August 18, 1962, Ringo Starr made his debut as the group's official drummer. Having signed a recording contract with EMI Records in England, the quartet shortened its name, and changed its spelling, to The Beatles, and began recording several of the most memorable songs of the 1960s.

A hit in England first, when the group made their American live television debut on "The Ed Sullivan Show" on February 9, 1964, the frenzy known as Beatlemania and the phenomenon known as the British Invasion were officially underway. With several albums already released in England, the American market was suddenly flooded with Beatles product. The week of April 4, the Beatles held the top five slots on *Billboard* magazine's "Hot 100" singles chart in the United States. Not only were The Beatles a hit on the airwaves, on television, and in concert, but that same year they also proved themselves as movie stars in the film *A Hard Day's Night*.

From 1964 to 1967, The Beatles and The Supremes seemed to rule the Number One slot on record charts on both sides of the Atlantic. They cranked out hit after hit, and as early as their 1966 album, *Revolver*, they began to display evidence of stretching out into new musical directions. When their 1967 masterpiece album, *Sgt. Pepper's Lonely Hearts Club Band,* hit the marketplace, The Beatles musically led the rest of the world into the psychedelic era. Later that year their BBC TV special, "Magical Mystery Tour," looked like a vivid LSD trip crossed with the Mad Hatter's tea party.

The group's 1968 double album, *The Beatles* (popularly known as The White Album), was recorded amid much grumbling about the possibility of the group breaking up. All of the members had established themselves as celebrities apart from The Beatles and began to move into different musical arenas. Although John Lennon's love affair with Japanese conceptual artist Yoko Ono is often blamed for the breakup of the group, the four members were simply growing in separate directions. The band thankfully stayed together long enough to produce another blockbuster album, *Abbey Road*.

In April of 1970, as The Beatles' *Let It Be* album was released, both McCartney and Starr released their first solo albums. On December 31, 1970, McCartney filed suit in England to dissolve the group legally. Throughout the 1970s, all four of The Beatles produced hit solo albums and singles. Paul McCartney formed a new band, called Wings, with his wife Linda. Ringo Starr had a string of million-selling singles, including "It Don't Come Easy" and "Photograph." George Harrison pioneered the all-star celebrity rock charity when he organized the Concert for Bangladesh in 1971. And John Lennon penned his brilliant signature song, "Imagine."

In 1980, only weeks after Lennon and Ono released their *Double Fantasy* album, Lennon was tragically gunned down in New York City, by a deranged fan. The rock world was in shock.

In 1994, the first new Beatles album to be released in two decades, *The Beatles Live at the BBC*, hit the stores. The recording instantly sold almost 5 million copies worldwide. In 1995, George, Paul, and Ringo went into a recording studio and added their music to a couple of newly discovered and John Lennon vocal tracks. Fifteen years after the death of John Lennon, The Beatles were heard together once again on the songs "Free as a Bird" and "Real Love."

The release of *Anthology 1* tipped off a whole new wave of Beatlemania, 90's style. A 2-CD set of rarities and outtakes from the very beginning of the group's career, the album entered the charts at Number One with first week sales figures in excess of 855,000 copies sold in America alone. The album was kicked off by a top-rated six hour television special broadcast over three nights. Twenty-five years after they had broken up, The Beatles ruled again. With all of their past rifts behind them, the three remaining Beatles once again entered Abbey Road studios together. According to Ringo, "We were four guys who really loved each other."

(Left to right) David Crosby, Stephen Stills, Graham Nash, and Neil Young in 1988

CROSBY, STILLS & NASH

(Crosby, Stills, Nash & Young releases noted with *; Crosby & Nash duet releases noted with **)

GROUP MEMBERS

David Crosby, Stephen Stills, Graham Nash, and occasionally Neil Young

BIGGEST HITS

- "Marrakesh Express" (1969)
- "Suite: Judy Blue Eyes" (1969)
- "Woodstock" (1970)*
- "Teach Your Children" (1970)*
- "Ohio" (1970)*
- "Our House" (1970)*
- "Immigration Man" (1972)**
- "Southbound Train" (1972)**

- "Carry Me" (1975)**
- "Out of the Darkness" (1976)**
- "Just a Song Before I Go" (1977)
- "Fair Game" (1977)
- "Wasted on the Way" (1982)
- "Southern Cross" (1982)
- "Too Much Love to Hide" (1983)
- "Got It Made" (1989)*

MILESTONE ALBUMS

- *Crosby, Stills & Nash* (1969)
- *Deja Vu* (1970)*
- *4 Way Street* (1971)*
- *Graham Nash/David Crosby* (1972)**
- *Wind on the Water* (1975)**
- *Whistling Down the Wire* (1976)**
- *Crosby/Nash—Live* (1977)**
- *CSN* (1977)
- *Daylight Again* (1982)
- *Allies* (1983)
- *American Dream* (1988)*
- *Live It Up* (1990)
- *After the Storm* (1994)

NOTABLE CD PACKAGES

- *So Far* [1 CD] (1974)*
- *Crosby, Stills & Nash* [4 CDs] (1991)

BAND HISTORY

When the trio of Crosby, Stills & Nash first united in 1969, they each brought to the "supergroup" years of singing and recording experience. David Crosby had been a member of the Byrds, Stephen Stills had been a member of Buffalo Springfield, and Graham Nash was fresh from the British group The Hollies. Almost immediately they became the hot new folk-rock band on the scene. Their debut album, *Crosby, Stills & Nash,* and subsequent August 1969 appearance at the Woodstock music festival, made them an instant hit. Hip, acoustic/electronic rock teamed with the trio's beautiful vocal harmonies won the group a Best New Artist Grammy Award, and a strong legion of fans that continues even today.

The career of Crosby, Stills & Nash has been high profile from the very start. Their first live gig was with Country Joe McDonald on July 25, 1969, at the Fillmore East in New York City. Their second live performance was on August 16 in Bethel, New York—at Woodstock in front of half a million people. They continued to tour through the winter, occasionally featuring their friend Joni Mitchell at some of the gigs (including Masonic Auditorium in Detroit).

In late 1969 they added another mutual friend to their lineup: ex–Buffalo Springfield member Neil Young. He performed live with the group at the infamous Altamont Speedway concert, which the Rolling Stones headlined (see "Beautiful People"). Neil was on hand for recording the group's most famous album, *Deja Vu.* The first Crosby, Stills, Nash & Young release, the band's single version of Joni Mitchell's "Woodstock," hit the charts in March 1970. Not only did the album hit Number One on the charts but it elevated the group's status through the roof. In June 1970, after watching a TV news report on the Kent State University "massacre" of four protesting students by the National Guard, Neil Young penned the song-of-the-troubled-times: "Ohio." It became a huge hit, and the group was viewed as being on the cutting edge of social consciousness, exposing society's problems through prophetic rock music.

At the height of their newly established fame, while on an American concert tour, the band members began arguing with each other. Stephen Stills was arrested for drug possession, and the band began having serious internal problems. In addition, Neil Young was blamed for causing further friction and dissension within the group.

At this point, all four of the group's members began to splinter off into various solo album projects.

In September of 1970, Neil Young released his second solo album, *After the Goldrush*, and that December, Stephen Stills released his first solo album, *Stephen Stills*, and had a big hit with the single "Love the One You're With." The following May, Crosby released his solo LP *If I Could Only Remember My Name*, and Nash did likewise in July with his *Songs for Beginners*. Meanwhile, in May of that year, Atlantic Records released the two-record live set, *4 Way Street*, by Crosby, Stills, Nash & Young. It immediately hit Number One and was ranked as the best live rock album recorded to date.

In 1972, two members of the group came back together again, with the release of the duet album *Graham Nash/David Crosby*. In June of the following year, Crosby, Stills, Nash & Young all met in Hawaii to work together on a projected reunion album. Meanwhile, several more solo albums were released, including two by Stills's new band, Manassas, and *Wild Tales* (1974) by Nash. By the summer of 1974, Crosby, Stills, Nash & Young were back on the road together, touring, and the "greatest hits" album, *So Far,* was released. Suddenly anticipation was high for all four group members to record in the studio again.

In January, 1975, while attempting to come up with a reunion album, Graham and Stephen got into a huge fight over a single note of music. Angered, Neil stormed out of the studio and vowed never to return again.

Two years and several solo and Nash/Crosby albums later, in 1977— without Neil Young—Crosby, Stills & Nash recorded a new album, *CSN*, and launched a vastly successful concert tour. The following year, they set out on a critically acclaimed "acoustic only" tour.

In September of 1979, Crosby, Stills & Nash were among the performers at the legendary MUSE concerts at Madison Square Garden, to protest the escalated use of nuclear power. They performed alongside Bruce Springsteen, the Doobie Brothers, Bonnie Raitt, James Taylor, Carly Simon, and a host of other rock stars. After that, the band members again went their separate ways, until 1983.

David Crosby was arrested twice in 1983: First in March, in Los Angeles, for drugs and carrying a concealed pistol, and then a month later for the same thing in Dallas, Texas. That fall the reunited trio released their album *Daylight Again,* and their prophetic drug song, "Wasted on the Way," became a huge radio hit. On August 5, 1983, David Crosby was convicted of cocaine possession and carrying a gun into the Texas bar he had been arrested in a few months earlier. In the mid-'80s Crosby went through mandatory drug rehabilitation and spent time in a Texas prison.

With Crosby "clean and sober" and the group finally burying the hatchet of their differences, Crosby, Stills, Nash & Young reunited in 1988 for the 14-track album *American Dream*, which included the hit single "Got It Made." Eventually Young returned to his solo projects, and the trio of Crosby, Stills & Nash released the album *Live It Up* in 1990.

In 1994, the trio released the album *After the Storm* and embarked on its historic 25th Anniversary concert tour. The tour, which began in May in Tucson, Arizona, included an appearance at Woodstock '94. Not long after that performance, David Crosby began having liver problems. His years of substance abuse had taken their toll, and he needed a liver transplant. He underwent the surgery and recovered well enough to perform live for a Grammy Awards reunion with Stills and Nash, on a quartet version of "Love the One You're With" with Luther Vandross.

Fleetwood Mac: *(Left to right)* Lindsey Buckingham, Christine McVie, Mick Fleetwood, Stevie Nicks, John McVie

FLEETWOOD MAC

MOST FAMOUS GROUP LINEUP

Mick Fleetwood, John McVie, Lindsey Buckingham, Christine McVie, Stevie Nicks

BIGGEST HITS

- "Oh Well—Pt. 1" (1970)
- "Over My Head" (1975)
- "Rhiannon (Will You Ever Win)" (1976)
- "Say You Love Me" (1976)
- "Go Your Own Way" (1977)
- "Dreams" (1977)
- "Don't Stop" (1977)
- "You Make Loving Fun" (1977)
- "Tusk" (1979)
- "Sara" (1979)

- "Think About Me" (1980)
- "Sisters of the Moon" (1980)
- "Fireflies" (1981)
- "Hold Me" (1982)
- "Gypsy" (1982)
- "Love in Store" (1982)
- "Big Love" (1987)
- "Little Lies" (1987)
- "Seven Wonders" (1987)
- "Everywhere" (1987)
- "Family Man" (1988)
- "Isn't It Midnight" (1988)
- "As Long as You Follow" (1989)
- "Save Me" (1990)

MILESTONE ALBUMS

- *Then Play On* (1969)
- *Kiln House* (1970)
- *Future Games* (1971)
- *Bare Trees* (1972)
- *Penguin* (1973)
- *Mystery to Me* (1973)
- *Heroes Are Hard to Find* (1974)
- *Fleetwood Mac* (1975)
- *Rumours* (1977)
- *Tusk* (1979)
- *Fleetwood Mac Live* (1980)
- *Mirage* (1982)
- *Tango in the Night* (1987)
- *Behind the Mask* (1990)
- *Time* (1995)

NOTABLE CD PACKAGES

- *Fleetwood Mac's Greatest Hits* [1 CD] (1988)
- *Fleetwood Mac: 25 Years—The Chain* [4 CDs] (1992)

BAND HISTORY

Fleetwood Mac went through eight years and ten incarnations before they hit the winning musical lineup that took them from being a cult blues band to becoming an international sensation. The band's 1977 album, *Rumours,* was Number One on the *Billboard* album chart for a record-breaking 31 weeks and eventually sold over 15 million copies worldwide. At the height of their fame, they were the best-selling rock band in the world.

Formed in England in 1967, Fleetwood Mac originally consisted of Mick Fleetwood on drums, Bob Brunning on bass, and Peter Green and Jeremy Spencer on guitar and vocals. Three months later Brunning left the band, and was replaced by bass player John McVie. It was this version that released the 1968 debut album, *Fleetwood Mac.* The band was an instant sensation in the United Kingdom and scored the hits "Albatross" (1968), "Man of the World" (1969), and "Oh Well—Pt. 1" (1970).

In 1970 John's wife, Christine McVie, joined the band on keyboard and vocals. She made her recording debut on the critically acclaimed album *Kiln House* (1970). When Fleetwood Mac released its 1971 album, *Future Games*, California musician Bob Welch joined the band on guitar and vocals, and his musical influence moved the group further away from its blues/rock base into more of an acoustic West Coast folk/rock sound. Throughout all of the band's lineup changes, Christine, John, and Mick would remain in Fleetwood Mac from the group's fifth through eleventh incarnations. Welch also remained with the band as they released four consecutively well received LPs: *Bare Trees* (1972), *Penguin* (1973), *Mystery to Me* (1973), and *Heroes Are Hard to Find* (1974).

In December 1974, Welch left the band, and a divine chance meeting resulted in creating the Fleetwood Mac lineup that was destined for rock immortality. Mick Fleetwood was touring a Los Angeles recording studio, with the idea of checking it out for his band's next album, when he ran into a pair of singer/songwriters he found interesting. They had recorded a relatively unknown but respected album, *Buckingham Nicks*. Fleetwood instantly liked the pair and asked them to join his band. With that Stevie Nicks and Lindsey Buckingham officially became an important element in the success of the tenth and most famous version of Fleetwood Mac.

With the McVies and Mick Fleetwood blending their British rock sensibilities with the California harmonies of Buckingham and Nicks, the result was sheer alchemy. The band's first album together, *Fleetwood Mac* (1975), became a huge Number One album and was the toast of the rock world.

When Christine and John's marriage, and the love affair of Stevie and Lindsey, both ended in 1976, the group was inspired to write some of rock's most important songs about love lost. The resulting *Rumours* album made Fleetwood Mac the biggest and most successful band in the world.

After producing the biggest-selling rock album in the history of recorded music, mega-commercial success presented a new set of pressures for the overnight superstar band: deciding how to follow it up. The resulting double-album, *Tusk* (1979), was uneven and over-produced. The band's record label tried to get the group to repeat the same musical formula as *Rumours*, but eclectic Lindsay Buckingham led the outfit into the self-indulgent direction of *Tusk*. The odd but fascinating album took two years and a million dollars to produce. It yielded two hit singles: "Sara" and the bizarre title track. The chantlike "Tusk" featured the U.S.C. Trojan Marching Band, which was recorded live in Dodger Stadium.

As eclectic as the *Tusk* album was, Fleetwood Mac still enjoyed its status as one of the biggest rock groups in the world. From October 26, 1979, in Pocatello, Idaho, in front of an audience of 13,000 to September 1, 1980, at the Hollywood Bowl in Los Angeles in front of an audience of 17,500, Fleetwood Mac toured the world. Along the way they recorded the well-received *Fleetwood Mac Live* album, released in December of 1980.

By this point in time, Fleetwood Mac was so famous that the individual group members were able to go off and record their own solo projects, and in 1981 that's what three of them did. Mick Fleetwood spent and lost a fortune recording an odd album called *The Visitor*, in Ghana, West Africa. Stevie scored a huge success with her first solo album, *Bella Donna*, and Lindsey had a hit with his solo project, *Law & Order*, which spawned the Top Ten single "Trouble."

Following a three-year hiatus recording as a band in the studio, Fleetwood Mac released *Mirage* in 1982. It was the group's first Number One album since *Rumours*, and it contained the hit singles "Hold Me," "Gypsy," and "Love in Store." For the next four years, the band went off in their own directions on further solo projects. Stevie released two more solo albums: *The Wild Heart* (1983) and *Rock a Little* (1985). Christine's first album, *The Christine Perfect Album* (1970), bore her maiden name of "Perfect" and established her as a solo star prior to joining Fleetwood Mac. In 1984 she released the brilliant album *Christine McVie*, which contained the hit singles "Got a Hold on Me" and "Love Will Show Us How." Meanwhile, embroiled in financial problems, Mick Fleetwood filed for bankruptcy on May 1, 1984. While all of this was going on, Lindsey was busy becoming a recluse in his Bel Air home.

In 1987, after four years apart, the band was still off on solo ventures. Christine was in the recording studio working on a version of Elvis Presley's "Can't Stop Falling in Love" for the soundtrack of the Blake Edwards movie *A Fine Mess*. She was having trouble getting the sound she wanted, so she contacted John McVie and Lindsey Buckingham to help. The result was an in-studio reunion for Fleetwood Mac, and ultimately the album *Tango in the Night*. Overdubbed and mixed at Lindsey's house, the album became the group's biggest seller since *Rumours*. When the band began planning a concert tour to support the album, Buckingham got cold feet and didn't want to tour. In July, while the group's single "Big Love" was in the Top Five in the U.S., Fleetwood Mac fired Lindsey Buckingham. In September, after the song "Seven Wonders" hit the Top 20, the band began "secret" Lindsey-less rehearsals with replacement members Billy Burnette and Rick Vito.

With the twelfth version of Fleetwood Mac (Mick Fleetwood, Christine McVie, John McVie, Stevie Nicks, Rick Vito, and Billy Burnette) cemented, the group embarked on their "Shake the Cage" tour of Europe and Australia. The album *Fleetwood Mac's Greatest Hits* was released in 1988 with 16 cuts—three of them new recordings—and it became a huge hit. In 1990 the band released *Behind the Mask* and launched the "Mask" tour. At the height of their rekindled fame, on September 7, 1990, the band played its last date, with Stevie Nicks and Christine McVie both announcing their departures from the group.

In 1992, the band released it's four-CD boxed-set, *Fleetwood Mac: 25 Years—The Chain*. Fans were thrilled when in January of 1993, after six years apart, the original members of Fleetwood Mac (John, Mick, Stevie, Christine, and Lindsey) reunited for a special network telecast, one-time-only performance at the inaugural celebration for U.S. President Bill Clinton. Eclectic and unpredictable, the band has continued to pursue projects apart. However, another reunion album and tour is always an anticipated possibility for Fleetwood Mac.

The group surprised their fans in 1995 with a fascinating new incarnation of the group with mainstays Mick Fleetwood, John McVie, and Christine McVie—plus Billy Burnette—joined by old/new member Dave Mason. For an additional female vocalist, the group enlisted young Bekka Bramlett, daughter of legendary rock singer Bonnie Bramlett, who was part of the duo Delaney & Bonnie. Together, the new version of Fleetwood Mac released the 1995 album *Time*. Despite the passage of time and the group's personnel changes, the saga of Fleetwood Mac continues to grow and evolve.

Aretha Franklin

ARETHA FRANKLIN
BIGGEST HIT SINGLES

- "I Never Loved a Man (the Way I Love You)" (1967)
- "Respect" (1967)
- "Baby I Love You" (1967)
- "A Natural Woman" (1967)
- "Chain of Fools" (1967)
- "(Sweet Sweet Baby) Since You've Been Gone" (1968)
- "Think" (1968)
- "The House That Jack Built" (1968)
- "I Say a Little Prayer" (1968)
- "Don't Play That Song" (1970)
- "Bridge Over Troubled Water" (1971)
- "Spanish Harlem" (1971)
- "Rock Steady" (1971)
- "Day Dreaming" (1972)
- "Until You Come Back to Me (That's What I'm Gonna Do)" (1973)
- "Something He Can Feel" (1976)
- "Jump to It" (1982)
- "Freeway of Love" (1985)
- "Who's Zoomin' Who?" (1985)
- "Sisters Are Doin' It for Themselves" [with Eurythmics] (1985)
- "Jumpin' Jack Flash" (1986)
- "I Knew You Were Waiting" [with George Michael] (1987)
- "Through the Storm" [with Elton John] (1989)
- "Everyday People" (1991)
- "A Deeper Love" (1994)

MILESTONE ALBUMS

- *The Tender, the Moving, the Swinging Aretha Franklin* (1962)
- *I Never Loved a Man the Way I Love You* (1967)
- *Aretha Arrives* (1967)
- *Aretha: Lady Soul* (1968)
- *Aretha Now* (1968)
- *Aretha Franklin: Soul '69* (1969)
- *Aretha Live at Fillmore West* (1971)
- *Young, Gifted and Black* (1972)
- *Sparkle* (1976)
- *Love All the Hurt Away* (1981)
- *Jump to It* (1982)
- *Who's Zoomin' Who* (1985)
- *Aretha* (1986)
- *Through the Storm* (1989)
- *What You See Is What You Sweat* (1991)

NOTABLE CD PACKAGES

- *Aretha Franklin: Jazz to Soul* [2 CDs] (1992)
- *Aretha Franklin: Queen of Soul* [4 CDs] (1992)
- *Aretha Franklin: Greatest Hits 1980–1994* [1 CD] (1994)

CAREER HISTORY

Aretha Franklin is known as the Queen of Soul. It is a title that she wears with regal pride. As one of the most enduring stars in musical history—forty years since she made her recording debut—she is still as vital a force in the music business as she was at the height of her initial success. Her recent hit singles, "A Deeper Love" and "Willing to Forgive," from 1994 will attest to that.

She began her singing career as a child in Detroit, Michigan, where people would come from miles around to listen to her sing in the choir of the New Bethel Baptist Church. At 14, Aretha Franklin's prodigy-like vocal talents were recorded on the 1956 album *Songs of Faith*. She had been taught to sing gospel by family friends Mahalia Jackson and Marion Williams but was highly influenced by another of her father's friends, Clara Ward.

In 1960, at 18, Franklin was signed to Columbia Records by John Hammond, who produced the last recordings by Bessie Smith and discovered Billie Holiday. Working with various producers, including Robert Mersey, famous for his work with Barbra Streisand, and Clyde Otis, producer of Dinah Washington's biggest hits, Aretha stayed with Columbia Records for seven years as a jazz singer.

In 1967, Franklin signed with Atlantic Records, teaming up with producers Jerry Wexler, Arif Mardin, and Tom Dowd to produce a solid decade of soulfully smashing hits, including "I Never Loved a Man (the Way I Love You)," "Respect," "A Natural Woman," "Think," "Ain't No Way," "The Weight," "I Say a Little Prayer," and "The House That Jack Built."

In the 1970s, Aretha Franklin became the media's black earth mother. Her albums *Young, Gifted and Black* and *Live at Fillmore West* captured both rock & roll and soul audiences, enabling her to win Grammy Awards for Best R&B Performance, Female, for eight consecutive years (1967 to 1974). Aretha's 1970s reign on the charts included "Rock Steady," "Angel," her red-hot version of "Spanish Harlem," and the Curtis Mayfield–produced "Something He Can Feel."

Franklin's career low point came in the late 1970s when she recorded a couple of disco concept and cabaret dance albums (*Almighty Fire* [1978] and *La Diva* [1979] respectively). It was when she signed with Arista Records, and company president Clive Davis, that she began to rebuild her floundering career. A pair of classy albums, *Aretha* in 1980 and *Love All the Hurt Away* in 1981, set the stage for her return to musical prominence. The following year, her version of Sam and Dave's "Hold On I'm Comin'" grabbed her another Grammy. She was on her way. For her next two albums she teamed up with a new producer, Luther Vandross, who penned the humorous Top 40 gem "Jump to It," and suddenly Aretha's career was jump-started back to life. The albums, *Jump to It* and *Get It Right*, were snappy, contemporary, and showed Franklin off at her most soulful.

In 1985, Franklin released her biggest-selling album yet, *Who's Zoomin' Who*, produced by Narada Michael Walden. Her smash single, "Freeway of Love," and its amusing video, were the hits of the summer of 1985. To enhance her audience appeal, Aretha began featuring duets with contemporary stars on her albums. Among the best have been "I Knew Your Were Waiting" with George Michael, "Through the Storm" with Elton John, "Sisters Are Doin' It for Themselves" with Annie Lennox and Dave Stewart of Eurythmics, "It Isn't, It Wasn't, It Ain't Never Gonna Be" with Whitney Houston, and "In These Changing Times" with Michael McDonald.

Elton John

ELTON JOHN
BIGGEST HITS

- "Your Song" (1970)
- "Levon" (1971)
- "Tiny Dancer" (1972)
- "Rocket Man" (1972)
- "Honky Cat" (1972)

- "Crocodile Rock" (1972)
- "Daniel" (1973)
- "Goodbye Yellow Brick Road" (1973)
- "Bennie and the Jets" (1974)
- "Don't Let the Sun Go Down on Me" (1974)
- "The Bitch Is Back" (1974)
- "Lucy in the Sky with Diamonds" (1974)
- "Philadelphia Freedom" (1975)
- "Someone Saved My Life Tonight" (1975)
- "Island Girl" (1975)
- "Sorry Seems to Be the Hardest Word" (1976)
- "Don't Go Breaking My Heart" [with Kiki Dee] (1976)
- "Mama Can't Buy You Love" (1979)
- "Little Jeannie" (1980)
- "Empty Garden (Hey Hey Johnny)" (1982)
- "Blue Eyes" (1982)
- "I Guess That's Why They Call It the Blues" (1983)
- "I'm Still Standing" (1983)
- "Kiss the Bride" (1983)
- "Sad Songs Say So Much" (1984)
- "Nikita" (1985)
- "Wrap Her Up" (1985)
- "I Don't Wanna Go on with You Like That" (1988)
- "A Word in Spanish" (1988)
- "Through the Storm" [with Aretha Franklin] (1989)
- "Healing Hands" (1989)
- "Sacrifice" (1990)
- "The Club at the End of the Street" (1990)
- "Don't Let the Sun Go Down on Me" [with George Michael] (1991)
- "The One" (1992)
- "True Love" [with Kiki Dee] (1993)

- "Can You Feel the Love Tonight" (1994)
- "Believe" (1995)

MILESTONE ALBUMS

- *Empty Sky* (1969)
- *Elton John* (1970)
- *Tumbleweed Connection* (1971)
- *11-17-70* (1971)
- *Madman Across the Water* (1971)
- *Honky Chateau* (1972)
- *Don't Shoot Me I'm Only the Piano Player* (1973)
- *Goodbye Yellow Brick Road* (1973)
- *Caribou* (1974)
- *Captain Fantastic and the Brown Dirt Cowboy* (1975)
- *Rock of the Westies* (1975)
- *Blue Moves* (1976)
- *A Single Man* (1978)
- *Victim of Love* (1979)
- *21 at 33* (1980)
- *The Fox* (1981)
- *Jump Up!* (1982)
- *Too Low for Zero* (1983)
- *Breaking Hearts* (1984)
- *Leather Jackets* (1986)
- *Live in Australia* (1987)
- *Reg Strikes Back* (1988)
- *Sleeping with the Past* (1989)
- *The One* (1992)
- *Duets* (1993)
- *Made in England* (1995)

NOTABLE CD PACKAGES

- *Elton John's Greatest Hits* [1 CD] (1974)
- *Elton John's Greatest Hits, Volume II* [1 CD] (1977)
- *Elton John's Greatest Hits, 1976–1986* [1 CD] (1992)
- *To Be Continued . . .* [4 CDs] (1990)

CAREER HISTORY

In a way, Elton John is one of rock & roll's most unlikely superstars. He doesn't have the overconfident swagger that characterizes Bruce Springsteen and Rod Stewart, but he always manages to touch us with his poignant lyrics and vocals, and entertains us with his outlandish sense of fashion. For much of his career, he has done his best to play the on-stage clown with his platform shoes, crazy hats, and over-the-top clothes. However, even in his most flamboyant moments, he still delivers the goods when it comes down to selling a song. 1995 Grammy and Academy awards for the 1994 hit single, "Can You Feel the Love Tonight" (from the film *The Lion King*) have given him renewed importance and stature, and have underscored the significance of his role in the rock world.

Even in his slump periods, Elton John continued to produce sometimes insightful, sometimes bawdy, and always interesting music. Born in London in 1947, Elton John joined a local R&B band called Bluesology when he was a teenager. With Elton as the group's keyboard player, the band's first major gig was performing for 18 months as the back-up band for a series of American R&B acts, including The Ink Spots, Patti LaBelle & the Bluebelles, Major Lance, and Doris Troy. In 1967, after a disastrous audition for a solo recording deal with Liberty Records, company executive Ray Williams passed John some lyrics written by a British lad named Bernie Taupin. So began one of the most fruitful professional music writing relationships of the 20th century.

John and Taupin found that they hit it off immensely well, and they set about to sell their initial compositions. In 1968 (having just changed his real name of Reginald Dwight to his stage name of Elton John) John recorded his first single, "I've Been Loving You Too Long," but it failed to hit the charts. Meanwhile, Roger Cook recorded the writing duo's "Skyline Pigeon." John then recorded his second single for Phillips Records, "Lady Samantha," and again it bombed. In America, Three Dog Night recorded "Lady Samantha" on its very successful *Suitable for Framing* album, and John and Taupin's music was exposed to a whole new audience. In 1969, Elton John's debut album, *Empty Sky,* was released. It comprised 100 percent of John and Taupin originals. However, it was his second album, *Elton John,* that established him on both sides of the Atlantic. Thanks to the Top Ten success of the hit single, "Your Song," the album hit the American Number Four on the album chart and was certified gold. The following year saw four new Elton John albums: *Tumbleweed Connection, Friends* (movie soundtrack), *11-17-70* (from a radio concert), and *Madman Across the Water.*

Suddenly, Elton John was *the* hot new rock balladeer on the scene. His 1972 hits, "Tiny Dancer" and "Rocket Man," propelled his *Honky Chateau* LP to the Number One spot in *Billboard* magazine. That album was to begin a streak of seven consecutive million-selling Number One albums. Suddenly everything he touched turned to gold. Amid his most consistent hit-making streak, from 1972 to 1976, John placed eight singles in the Top Five, including "Goodbye Yellow Brick Road," "Bennie and the Jets," "Don't Let the Sun Go Down on Me," "The Bitch Is Back," "Lucy in the Sky with Diamonds," "Philadelphia Freedom," "Someone Saved My Life Tonight," and "Island Girl."

In 1975, Elton John became the first white performer to be invited to perform on the American television program "Soul Train." The following year, he was immortalized in wax at Madame Tussaud's in London, and he was one of the rock stars to appear in Ken Russell's vivid film version of The Who's rock opera, *Tommy.* Appearing in a spangled outfit, and gigantic platform shoes, Elton portrayed the character of the Pinball Wizard.

After the release of his 1976 double album, *Blue Moves,* Elton broke form. It would be the last album entirely written by John and Taupin for a while. In 1978 he released *A Single Man,* his first album without any assistance from Bernie Taupin. It became his third consecutive platinum album in America. In 1979 John released an EP, *The Thom Bell Sessions,* containing three songs that he had recorded with the famed Philadelphia producer named in its title. From that disk, John scored his first Top Ten hit in three years, "Mama Can't Buy You Love."

Later that year, he released what can best be described as his "disco" album, *Victim of Love,* which was produced by Pete Bellotte, known for his work with Donna Summer. The title song became a sizeable hit for John.

In 1980, Elton released his 21st album, at the age of 33, hence the disk's title, *21 at 33.* It contained the hit single "(Sartorial Eloquence) Don't Ya Wanna Play This Game No More?" He signed a new deal with Geffen Records and produced four arty albums: *The Fox* (1981), *Jump Up!* (1982), *Too Low for Zero* (1983), and *Breaking Hearts* (1984). *Too Low for Zero* marked his first full-album reunion with Bernie Taupin since *Blue Moves,* and it yielded the hit "That's Why They Call It the Blues."

In the 1980s the music business experienced a sudden shift in marketing, as MTV began broadcasting. Jumping right into the video genre, Elton John's 1983 video for "I'm Still Standing" made him an instant hit with the first MTV generation. In 1986, John joined Gladys Knight and Stevie Wonder as "guests" on Dionne Warwick's single "That's What Friends Are For." The Burt Bacharach/Carole Bayer Sager song went on to become a huge Number One hit, raised a fortune for AIDS research, and won a Grammy for the foursome as the Best Pop Performance by a Group.

In 1987, Elton returned to MCA Records with his concert album, *Live in Australia,* complete with a whole symphony orchestra. On the album, he presented lush versions of several of his early classics, including "I Need You to Turn To," "Take Me to the Pilot," and "The Greatest Discovery." That same year, his live version of "Candle in the Wind" hit Number Six in the United States and Number Five in the United Kingdom.

In September 1988, after two decades of collecting outrageous eye-glasses and costumes, Elton John put 2,000 of his personal items and costumes on the auction block at Sotheby's in London. Later that month, John played the last of five nights at Madison Square Garden, which gave him a career total of twenty-six sold-out concerts at that venue—breaking the previous box-office record, set by the Grateful Dead.

Elton John's personal life, usually kept under wraps, was an ongoing subject of speculation. He was married to Renate Blauer from 1983 to 1987, but it seemed to be a totally passionless relationship. In 1988, British tabloid, *The Sun,* caused a scandal when it carried news of John being entangled with a male prostitute. John later sued, winning a million pounds in damages. The scandal did nothing to dim his superstar wattage, as he and Aretha Franklin scored a huge hit with the 1989 duet "Through the Storm." That September, he released *Sleeping with the Past,* which included the hits "Healing Hands" and "Sacrifice." The whole issue of Elton's sex life came to a head when he admitted in *Rolling Stone* magazine, in a very matter-of-fact fashion, that he was indeed gay. Instead of losing any of his fan base, he was saluted for his honesty.

In the 1990s Elton John is a revered rock & roll institution. He released the four-CD boxed set, *To Be Continued . . . ,* and the following year an all-star salute to Elton John and Bernie Taupin, *Two Rooms,* was released. The salute featured such stellar rock stars as Hall and Oates, Tina Turner, The Beach Boys, Eric Clapton, Rod Stewart, The Who, and Sting, each singing John/Taupin classics. In 1993, on his album *Duets,* John was heard singing with still another list of rock heroes, which included Bonnie Raitt, Tammy Wynette, George Michael, k.d. lang, RuPaul, and Kiki Dee.

Adding his songs to the 1994 Disney film *The Lion King* delivered his music to still another generation of fans. When it came time for the 1995 Oscar nominations, three of Elton John's songs from the animated feature were included in the list of Best Song nominees. In March of 1995, John's *Lion King* song "Can You Feel the Love Tonight" netted him not only a Grammy Award but his first Oscar as well. That same month he released his new *Made in England,* which produced the hit single "Believe." Obviously, after 25 years at the top of the charts, Elton John has only just begun!

Madonna

MADONNA

NUMBER ONE SINGLES

- "Like a Virgin" (1984)
- "Crazy for You" (1985)
- "Live to Tell" (1986)
- "Papa Don't Preach" (1986)
- "Open Your Heart" (1987)
- "Who's That Girl" (1987)
- "Like a Prayer" (1989)
- "Vogue" (1990)
- "Justify My Love" (1990)

- "This Used to Be My Playground" (1992)
- "Take a Bow" (1995)

MILESTONE ALBUMS

- *Madonna* (1983)
- *Like a Virgin* (1984)
- *True Blue* (1986)
- *Who's That Girl* (1987)
- *You Can Dance* (1987)
- *Like a Prayer* (1989)
- *I'm Breathless* (1990)
- *Erotica* (1992)
- *Bedtime Stories* (1994)
- *Something to Remember* (1995)

NOTABLE CD PACKAGE

- *The Immaculate Collection* [1 CD] (1990)

CAREER HISTORY

Madonna has had one of the most unique and exciting careers in rock & roll history. Instead of following in the footsteps of any existing fore-runners, she has almost single-handedly fashioned an ever-changing career for herself. Singer, writer, actress, and pouting sex goddess, she has created an image for herself as a virtual dominatrix. To her, vulner-ability is a charade to mask her cold-as-steel motives.

While sweet and sentimental songs like "Rain," "Take a Bow," "This Used to Be My Playground," and "Crazy for You" have brought her great success, her songs of blatant sexuality like "Erotica," "Justify My Love," "Hanky Panky," "Material Girl," "Express Yourself," and "Like a Virgin" more closely reflect her ever-controversial public image.

Born in Pontiac, Michigan, in 1958, Madonna moved to New York City in 1977 with visions of stardom in her head and $35 in her pocket. Attractive, sexy, and streetwise, Madonna wasted no time climbing her way to the top. Her first goal was to become a dancer. When that aspiration only yielded a spot on a second-string company of the Alvin Ailey Dancers, she redirected her focus toward becoming a singer. Whatever limitations she may have had vocally, she made up for in moxie.

Madonna had been lucky in that she was able to capitalize on the kindness of useful friends and boyfriends. Singer/writer Dan Gilroy (The Breakfast Club) taught her about performance rock, disco D.J. Mark Kamins landed her a recording deal, and John "Jellybean" Benitez introduced her to the upper echelon of the record business. Her initial hits, "Borderline," "Holiday," and "Lucky Star," were aimed at the post-disco dance audience, and in New York City and London she became an instant smash. Since her career came together just in time for the beginning of MTV, Madonna's unique fashion look and ability to dance made her the video network's darling. In September of 1984, Madonna performed a choreographed live version of her about-to-be-released new single, "Like a Virgin," on the First Annual MTV Awards telecast. She performed the song in yards of wedding dress tulle and ended by writhing around on the stage floor of Radio City Music Hall, and finally dry-humping the floor. Weeks later, the single, the album, and the video of "Like a Virgin" became instant smashes.

In January 1985, Madonna filmed the video of her next single, "Material Girl," aping Marilyn Monroe's famed "Diamonds Are a Girl's Best Friend" number from *Gentlemen Prefer Blondes*. On the set she met Brat-Pack actor Sean Penn. So began one of the "weirdest marriages" in rock history (see "The Chapel of Love"). In February, the movie *Vision Quest* was released, with a Madonna singing performance in it (she is seen in a nightclub scene). In March she was the star of her own feature film, *Desperately Seeking Susan*, with Rosanna Arquette. With three separate record labels involved, Madonna found herself with four different hits competing for space on the charts, including "Crazy for You" from *Vision Quest* and "Into the Groove" from *Desperately Seeking Susan*.

When young teenage girls suddenly started dressing to look like Madonna—complete with row after row of black rubber bracelets and several crucifixes dangling from every appendage—the singer became ubiquitous. In the spring of 1985, *Time* magazine put

Madonna on its cover, and almost instantly she was the year's biggest star.

That summer, when she was at the height of her notoriety, *Playboy* and *Penthouse* magazines announced that in their upcoming issues they would feature photos of Madonna nude. However, throwing bad publicity at brash Madonna was like trying to put out a fire with gasoline. An appearance at the mega-charity concert, Live Aid, and her three-ring circus marriage to Sean Penn pushed her celebrity status through the roof. She ended the year with her *Like a Virgin* album certified multiple platinum and the song "Dress You Up" in the Top Ten.

Madonna's follow-up album, *True Blue,* was an instant smash, containing the ballad "Live to Tell" and "Papa Don't Preach," the controversial song about an unwed teenager's pregnancy. However, it wasn't long before Sean Penn became the thorn in her rosy publicity. He seemed to loathe having his photograph taken by the dozens of paparazzi swarming around him and his wife, while she loved the attention. When Penn took to beating up photographers, it was a tip-off that his violent temper would eventually erode their marriage.

After her fun and natural performance in *Desperately Seeking Susan*, Madonna proceeded to release one dreadful cinematic bomb after another, including *Shanghai Surprise*, *Who's That Girl*, and *Bloodhounds of Broadway*. Although the critics hated her, she held her own on Broadway in 1988, starring with Joe Mantagna and Ron Silver in David Mamet's *Speed the Plow*. Although her acting was flat, she kept racking up a steady string of hits, "Causing a Commotion," "Who's That Girl," and "La Isla Bonita" among them.

In 1989 she came up with another publicity explosion. In rapid succession, Madonna divorced Sean, hinted at a lesbian relationship with comedienne Sandra Bernhard, and began having an affair with Warren Beatty. She was then signed to play Breathless Mahoney in Beatty's screen production of *Dick Tracy*. While all of this was going on, she released her fifth album, *Like a Prayer*, complete with a video in which she dances in nothing but a slip in front of three KKK burning crosses, makes love to a black man in a church, and sings with a gospel choir.

Dick Tracy gave Madonna her finest screen moments to date. As an unscrupulous chorus girl who uses her sex appeal to get whatever she wants, she was perfect. While *Dick Tracy* was on the screen in theaters, Madonna was on tour with her Blonde Ambition stage show.

Using performance footage with candid backstage sequences, Madonna was the star and egocentric center of attention in the 1991 rock documentary film *Truth or Dare*. In it she was cursing, crying, bitching, and even giving "head" to a water bottle. In other words, she was seen as the most bizarre on-screen character of her entire film career.

In 1992, Madonna again delivered a strong film performance, as a 1940s female baseball player, alongside Geena Davis and Rosie O'Donnell in *A League of Their Own*. However, that fall Madonna pushed the envelope of taste a bit too far when she released her first book, *Sex*, and her next album, *Erotica*. The *Sex* book featured passages of Madonna describing her genitalia and what it is like to masturbate; nude photos of her with men, women, dogs, and drag queens; and several sex-crazed fantasy passages. Retailing for $50, the book was an immediate best-seller. The *Erotica* album, however, proved to be just a bit too much. While the title song was fun, Madonna's songs about oral sex and her own glorious vagina were a little over the top. The one real hit from the album was the subtle love song, "Rain."

In 1994, Madonna released one of her most fascinating departure albums, *Bedtime Stories*. A mix of ballads, hip-hop, and space-age '90s rock, it demonstrated her ability to be directed by outside record producers, and it showed her at her most musically challenging. It featured the hits "Secret," "Take a Bow," and the Björk-penned "Bedtime Stories." In 1995, when "Take a Bow" hit Number One, Madonna became the solo female rock star with the greatest number of chart-topping hits. Like a chameleon, Madonna continues to grow and adapt herself to a limitless wealth of creative projects, brilliantly and scandalously publicized by her own private antics.

At long last, in 1995, Madonna's cinematic dream came true, and she began filming the operatically sung screen version of the Broadway hit *Evita*. Portraying Argentina's goddess, Eva Perón, Madonna found her ultimate on-screen challenge. And to further distance herself from the slut-kitten image she created for the *Erotica* album, Madonna released her all-ballad retrospective LP *Something to Remember* and the hit "You'll See."

Joni Mitchell

JONI MITCHELL
BIGGEST HITS

- "Big Yellow Taxi" (1970)
- "Carey" (1971)
- "You Turn Me on I'm a Radio" (1972)
- "Raised on Robbery" (1974)
- "Help Me" (1974)
- "Free Man in Paris" (1974)

- "Big Yellow Taxi" [live version] (1974)
- "In France They Kiss on Main Street" (1976)
- "(You're So Square) Baby, I Don't Care" (1982)
- "Good Friends" [with Michael McDonald] (1986)

MILESTONE ALBUMS

- *Joni Mitchell* (1968)
- *Clouds* (1969)
- *Ladies of the Canyon* (1970)
- *Blue* (1971)
- *For the Roses* (1972)
- *Court and Spark* (1974)
- *Miles of Aisles* (1974)
- *The Hissing of Summer Lawns* (1975)
- *Hejira* (1976)
- *Don Juan's Reckless Daughter* (1977)
- *Mingus* (1979)
- *Shadows and Light* (1980)
- *Wild Things Run Fast* (1982)
- *Dog Eat Dog* (1985)
- *Chalk Mark in a Rain Storm* (1988)
- *Night Ride Home* (1991)
- *Turbulent Indigo* (1994)

CAREER HISTORY

Joni Mitchell is the ultimate female folk troubadour. For four decades she has personified the role of an arty, sophisticated, socially conscious folk/rock singer. Joni first came to prominence as a songwriter, and she gained national attention when her song "Both Sides Now" was recorded in 1968 by Judy Collins, for whom it was a Top Ten hit.

Her first album, *Joni Mitchell* (1968), was produced by David Crosby, and her affiliation with his group—Crosby, Stills, Nash & Young—has been a thread throughout her career. The quartet recorded "Woodstock," her ode to the rock festival, and several times she toured with the group as their opening act.

Her second album, *Clouds* (1969), featured Joni's distinctive versions of her songs "Chelsea Morning" and "Both Sides Now." The following year, the album won her a Grammy Award for Best Folk Performance, Female. While sharing a house with Graham Nash, Joni recorded her third album, *Ladies of the Canyon,* which features her interpretation "The Circle Game" and her own haunting version of "Woodstock."

These four songs by Joni—"Both Sides Now," "Circle Game," "Chelsea Morning," and "Woodstock"—carried fresh nuances when recorded by Mitchell herself. Covered by so many other recording artists previously, Joni's recordings were considered the ultimate versions. Joni was swept up in the whole troubadour movement, which also catapulted Carole King and Carly Simon to prominence.

Her 1971 album, *Blue,* is considered to be her most brilliant acoustic recording. To this day it is a steadily selling CD, which is considered a sheer classic of the singer/songwriter genre. After a year's vacation from her career, Joni returned to the marketplace with *For the Roses,* her first album for David Geffen's Asylum Records. It was this album that brought Joni her first Top 25 hit, "You Turn Me on I'm a Radio."

Throughout these formative years, Joni continued to establish her reputation for being an incredibly gifted singer/songwriter who had yet to break through to widespread fame. That all changed with her 1974 album, *Court and Spark.* By blending her trademark acoustic guitar and piano playing with a top-notch electric and jazz rock band, she had broken through with her most commercial and appealing recording yet. Aided by the chart hits "Help Me" and "Free Man in Paris," the recording became her first huge, Top Ten album. It also garnered her another Grammy Award, for Best Arrangement Accompanying Vocalists, on the song "Down to You."

That same year she released her first live album, *Miles of Aisles,* which included two new songs, "Jericho" and "Love or Money." The live version of her classic, "Big Yellow Taxi," went on to become a big chart hit for her. During the following two years she released two more masterful albums, *The Hissing of Summer Lawns* (1975) and the jazz-influenced *Hejira* (1976).

During this period, Joni was seen in several high-profile rock & roll contexts, including Bob Dylan's famed tour, the Rolling Thunder Revue, and the Band's feature-film farewell performance, *The Last Waltz*.

Over the years Joni continued to stretch and grow musically. She delved heavily into jazz with her albums *Don Juan's Reckless Daughter, Mingus,* and *Shadows and Light.* The unfolding of her association with Charles Mingus is a fascinating one. Stricken with Lou Gehrig's disease, jazz star Mingus enlisted Mitchell to put lyrics to several of his songs, and to ultimately assure his musical immortality with a wider audience of fans. She spent time with Mingus and added poignant lyrics to four of his songs. Inspired by his creativity, she added two of her own "Mingus-inspired" compositions. The resulting album, *Mingus,* features some of the most adventurous and complex music of her career. Released just months after the death of the jazz great, *Mingus* won her critical acclaim from some and questioning scorn from others. Devotees of pure jazz were apalled by the idea that a hippie folk singer could suddenly consider herself a jazz artist of the same calibre as Charles Mingus. This was the beginning of her somewhat thorny relationship with the press. Her concert tour late that year gave birth to her excellent live double album *Shadows and Light.* The music on it emerged like a cross between a historic jazz performance and an eclectic rock concert. Players on the album include Pat Metheny, Michael Brecker, and Jaco Pastorius.

In the 1980s, Joni's creative output continued as she signed a recording contract with Geffen Records and released her 1982 album *Wild Things Run Fast,* an introspective disk on which she returned to a style that was closer to her folk and pop roots. It included her hit version of Elvis Presley's "(You're So Square) Baby, I Don't Care." Although this song became her biggest chart hit in almost a decade (number 47), it didn't achieve the kind of rock success that she had hoped. The album is noted for Joni's reproachment of pop music and a longing to capture her nostalgic love for the music of her youth.

On her 1985 album, *Dog Eat Dog,* Joni tried her hand at industrial/folk. In her quest to get involved in electronic synthesizer rock, she involved techno artist Thomas Dolby, who ultimately became co-producer of the album. Long acknowledged as being rock music's conscience, Joni recorded songs that blisteringly criticized current topics, including the thievery of televangelists ("Tax Free"), mass-media manipulation ("Fiction"), and the politics of the starving in Africa

("Ethiopia"). She proved that her socially conscious lyrics had lost none of their sting. Ultimately, *Dog Eat Dog* has become heralded as Joni's most sustained folk recording.

In 1988 she released her 15th album, *Chalk Mark in a Rainstorm*, which featured an all-star supporting cast including Peter Gabriel, Willie Nelson, Tom Petty, Wendy and Lisa, Don Henley, Thomas Dolby, and Billy Idol. In 1988 Joni was one of the star performers in Pink Floyd's historic staging of their rock opera *The Wall*, in front of the Berlin Wall in Germany.

Throughout the years, Joni's very expressive artwork graced the covers of most of her albums. She became so revered as an artist that she even became chummy with legendary artist Georgia O'Keefe, toward the end of the famed painter's long and fruitful life. Joni's friendship with O'Keefe deepened her interest in painting and strengthened her desire to be taken seriously as a painter. On the cover of her 17th album, *Turbulent Indigo*, Joni included her Van Gogh–esque self-portrait—with her missing right ear bandaged a la Vincent.

Her 1990s albums, *Night Ride Home* (1991) and *Turbulent Indigo* (1994), both find her as classy and intricate as always. Showing up in unexpected places, Joni Mitchell appearances have increased in the mid-'90s. Noteworthy recent performances have included an electrifying concert at the Edmonton Folk Festival in the summer of 1994 and a critically acclaimed broadcast concert in January of 1995. In her fourth decade of recording, Joni Mitchell remains as creative and insightful as always with her singing and her writing.

The Monkees: *(Left to right)* Peter Tork, Micky Dolenz, Davy Jones, Mike Nesmith

THE MONKEES

GROUP MEMBERS

Micky Dolenz, Davy Jones, Michael Nesmith, Peter Tork

BIGGEST HITS

- "Last Train to Clarksville" (1966)
- "I'm a Believer" (1966)

- "(I'm Not Your) Steppin' Stone" (1966)
- "A Little Bit Me, a Little Bit You" (1967)
- "Pleasant Valley Sunday" (1967)
- "Words" (1967)
- "Daydream Believer" (1967)
- "Valleri" (1968)
- "Randy Scouse Git" [Alternate Title] (1968) (Number Two British hit)
- "D. W. Washburn" (1968)
- "Porpoise Song" [from *Head*] (1968)
- "Listen to the Band" (1969)
- "That Was Then, This Is Now" (1986)
- "Heart and Soul" (1987)

NUMBER ONE ALBUMS

- *The Monkees* (1966) [Number One for 13 weeks]
- *More of the Monkees* (1967) [Number One for 18 weeks]
- *Headquarters* (1967) [Number One for 1 week]
- *Pisces, Aquarius, Capricorn & Jones Ltd.* (1967) [Number One for 5 weeks]

NOTABLE ALBUMS

- *The Birds, the Bees & the Monkees* (1968)
- *Head* [movie soundtrack] (1968)
- *Instant Replay* (1969)
- *The Monkees' Greatest Hits* [original version] (1969)
- *The Monkees Present* (1969)
- *Changes* (1970)

NOTABLE CD PACKAGES

- *Then and Now . . . The Best of the Monkees* [1 CD] (1986)
- *Listen to the Band* [4 CDs] (1991)

BAND HISTORY

The Monkees were patterned quite directly after The Beatles. Unlike The Beatles, however, it wasn't the forces of nature that originally brought Micky, Davy, Mike, and Peter together in 1965, but a television network. The initial idea popped into the heads of two Hollywood producers, Bob Rafelson and Bert Schneider, and a casting call was held. It was their concept to assemble four twenty-something young men and give them their own TV sitcom aimed directly at the teenaged rock & roll audience. The Beatles had scored cinematic success with their films *Help!* and *A Hard Day's Night*—why not replicate the jump-cut formula of both of those films and intersperse it with rock songs that could be popped in and out of episodes whenever needed?

Two of the group's members were actors who could sing, and two were singers who could act. Micky Dolenz was a child actor in the 1950s when he starred in his own television show, "Circus Boy." Davy Jones had played the Artful Dodger in the West End and Broadway productions of the hit musical *Oliver.* Mike and Peter were primarily folk-rock singers with lively personalities.

When the television show debuted on September 12, 1966, the group almost instantly became rock stars, with fans as avid as The Beatles'. For the most part, their first two albums were the product of a group of New York City songwriters under contract to musical director Don Kirshner. The songwriters included Carole King, Gerry Goffin, Neil Diamond, Neil Sedaka, and Tommy Boyce and Bobby Hart. The LPs *The Monkees* and *More of the Monkees* sold millions, but group members—particularly Mike and Peter—felt that the group was talented enough to produce its own music, without the studio musicians that gave them their initial hit sound. The result of this conflict was the firing of Kirshner and the creation of the group's own handcrafted album, *Headquarters.*

The television show lasted for two seasons, and the group breathed the rarefied air of international pop stardom. After the TV show ran its gamut, a television special, "33 1/3 Revolutions Per Monkee," and a movie, *Head,* were produced. The 1968 albums, *The Birds, the Bees & The Monkees* and the *Head* soundtrack, marked the group's last releases as a quartet. From that point forward, the band became a dwindling party. Peter left in December 1968, and a trio version of the Monkees released the albums *Instant Replay* (1969) and *The Monkees Present* (1969). In 1970 Mike quit, and Davy and Micky released the last successive Monkees album, *Changes,* as a duet. At that point the final two members of the group went their separate ways.

In 1986, MTV broadcast all 56 episodes of the original Monkees TV series, and tipped off one of the most successful reunions in rock history. Although Mike Nesmith declined rejoining the band, Micky, Davy, and Peter were on hand for several successful concert tours, and the hit albums *Then and Now . . . The Best of the Monkees* (1986) and *Pool It!* (1987). In August of 1986, there was a record number of seven Monkees albums on the *Billboard* album charts!

In 1989 the group again parted company, and in the 1990s both Jones and Dolenz separately penned their autobiographies. Micky's, *I'm a Believer: My Life of Music, Monkees, and Madness,* was the bigger success. In 1991 Rhino Records assembled a fabulous four-CD boxed-set retrospective on the group, called *Listen to the Band,* and in 1994 and 1995 Rhino released all nine of the original albums complete with rarities and outtakes. In 1995 there was talk about a new Monkees movie, album, and tour, in time for the 30th anniversary of the group.

Elvis Presley

ELVIS PRESLEY

NUMBER ONE HITS

- "Heartbreak Hotel" (1956)

- "I Want You, I Need You, I Love You" (1956)

- "Don't Be Cruel" (1956)

- "Hound Dog" (1956)

- "Love Me Tender" (1956)

- "Too Much" (1957)

- "All Shook Up" (1957)

- "(Let Me Be Your) Teddy Bear" (1957)
- "Jailhouse Rock" (1957)
- "Don't" (1958)
- "Hard Headed Woman" (1958)
- "A Big Hunk o' Love" (1958)
- "Stuck on You" (1959)
- "It's Now or Never" (1960)
- "Are You Lonesome Tonight" (1960)
- "Surrender" (1961)
- "Good Luck Charm" (1962)
- "Suspicious Minds" (1969)

Milestone Albums

- *Elvis Presley* (1956)
- *Elvis* (1956)
- *Loving You* (1956)
- *Elvis's Golden Records* (1958)
- *G.I. Blues* (1960)
- *Blue Hawaii* (1961)
- *Roustabout* (1964)
- *Elvis* [TV Special Soundtrack] (1968)
- *Aloha from Hawaii via Satellite* (1973)

Notable CD Packages

- *Elvis: The King of Rock 'n' Roll—The Complete '50s Masters* [5 CDs] (1992)
- *Elvis Presley—From Nashville to Memphis—The Essential '60s Remasters I* [5 CDs] (1993)

CAREER HISTORY

Elvis has always been the King of Rock & Roll. The excitement, the energy, the sneer, the gold lamé suit, and the pelvic thrusts made Elvis Presley the biggest rock star of the 1950s. He helped to define the whole phenomenon known as rock & roll.

Borrowing the intense theatrics of his peers—including Little Richard, Chuck Berry, and Jerry Lee Lewis—Elvis had a way of making love to a microphone stand. His initial hits, "Hound Dog," "Heartbreak Hotel," "(Let Me Be Your) Teddy Bear," and "Love Me Tender," still rank highest among the most appealing recordings of the entire rock & roll era.

Looking back on Elvis's life, it was really divided up into three distinct career phases. There was his initial burst of success from 1956 to 1959. His second phase spanned his 1960 release from the U.S. Army up to his 1968 television special. The third phase of his career, from 1969 to 1977, was his sad downward spiral, culminating in his tragic death at the age of 42.

Like so many kings, Elvis Presley—the King of Rock & Roll—came from humble beginnings. Born on January 8, 1935, to Vernon and Gladys Presley, he came into the world in his parents' two-room house in Tupelo, Mississippi. It was a tiny house that Vernon and his father built themselves. This is where the Presley musical legend all began. Who would have guessed that Elvis would have gone from that little two-room shed to his shrinelike mansion, Graceland, in Memphis, Tennessee.

After a short tenure at Sun Records in the early 1950s, his first RCA single, "Heartbreak Hotel," was released in 1956, and rock & roll would never be the same! Elvis wasn't the world's first rock star—but he was the first singing star to popularize the sound of rock & roll music with a combination of sexual urgency, unabashed emotionalism, and soulful angst. His sneering upper lip, uninhibited strut, and controversial pelvic thrusts caused young girls to swoon.

Elvis was also one of the first performers to effectively use television exposure to launch his single releases, and his career. Although America's television networks didn't have the slightest idea what to do with him—he became TV's first rock star. His first American national television appearance was on Tommy and Jimmy Dorsey's "Stage Show" in January 1956. Looking back on his first couple of TV guest spots, one has to admit that they were embarrassingly handled. Presley found himself trapped in silly comedy skits on "The Milton Berle Show," dressed uncomfortably in a tuxedo and tails on "The Steve Allen Show," and filmed from the waist up on "The Ed Sullivan Show." However hard they tried, the networks could not masquerade his sex appeal.

That very same year, while Number One hits "I Want You, I Need You, I Love You," "Don't Be Cruel," and "Hound Dog" were still hot on the charts, Elvis was already plotting his movie career. He made his film debut that very year in the western *Love Me Tender.* He also made his Las Vegas debut in 1956, at the Frontier Hotel.

On March 26, 1958, Elvis Presley's career was abruptly put on hold when he was drafted into the United States Army. Elvis, otherwise known as Private US 53310761, arrived in Germany on October 1, 1958, where he was stationed until early 1960. While he was in the army, his record label, RCA, which had cleverly stockpiled enough recordings, kept a steady flow of Elvis releases on the charts in his absence.

For the majority of the 1960s, Elvis mainly concentrated on his budding movie career, which included a record number of 33 films (see "Every Elvis Presley Movie").

Although he continued to tour and record in the 1970s, Elvis's final years represent one of the saddest chapters of rock history. His weight ballooned, and his shifted career thrust found him becoming a flashy jumpsuit-clad Las Vegas version of his former self. Disillusioned, and in a drugged fog of prescription pills, his last days were active, but hollow. At the time of his death in August of 1977, Elvis Presley had racked up over a dozen Number One hits and had placed 149 separate singles on *Billboard* magazine's "Hot 100" chart. Fortunately his 1950s and 1960s recordings, movies, and concert footage preserve the excitement that was Elvis Presley—the King of Rock & Roll.

Bonnie Raitt

BONNIE RAITT
BIGGEST HITS

- "Runaway" (1977)

- "You're Gonna Get What's Coming" (1979)

- "Thing Called Love" (1989)

- "Love Letter" (1989)

- "Nick of Time" (1990)

- "Let's Give Them Something to Talk About" (1991)

- "Not the Only One" (1992)

- "You Got It" (1995)
- "Rock Steady" (1995)

MILESTONE ALBUMS

- *Bonnie Raitt* (1971)
- *Give It Up* (1972)
- *Takin' My Time* (1973)
- *Streetlights* (1974)
- *Home Plate* (1975)
- *Sweet Forgiveness* (1977)
- *The Glow* (1979)
- *Green Light* (1982)
- *Nine Lives* (1986)
- *Nick of Time* (1989)
- *Luck of the Draw* (1991)
- *Longing in Their Hearts* (1994)
- *Road Tested* (1995)

NOTABLE CD PACKAGE

- *The Bonnie Raitt Collection* [1 CD] (1990)

CAREER HISTORY

Bonnie Raitt has had one of the longest roads toward success of any major rock performer today. Although she drew acclaim and a cult of die-hard fans through nine albums and 15 years at Warner Brothers records, it wasn't until 1989's 5-million-selling *Nick of Time* LP that she really broke through to mainstream stardom.

Long heralded as a top-notch musician, in the 1970s she experienced a career high point with the Top 40 single "Runaway" and the gold albums *Sweet Forgiveness* and *The Glow.* However, she is currently amid the most exciting string of successes of her career: Since 1990 she has released three successive multiple-platinum albums and racked up the phenomenal total of eight Grammy Awards.

Born the only daughter of Broadway singing star John Raitt, who starred in the original stage musicals of *Oklahoma* and *The Pajama Game,* Bonnie grew up in a musical family. Her mother played the piano, her brothers became musicians, and Bonnie gravitated toward the guitar. Her first idol was top folk troubadour Joan Baez. However, it was in college that Bonnie became fascinated by the blues.

While attending Radcliffe College in Massachusetts, Bonnie began dating musician Dick Waterman, who introduced her to blues legends Otis Rush, Fred McDowell, Son House, and Sippie Wallace. She quit college and began playing in New York City coffeehouses like the Gaslight. In 1971 she released her first album, *Bonnie Raitt,* which consisted of a blues-flavored repertoire comprised of classic Motown (the Marvelettes' "Danger Heartbreak Dead Ahead"), current '70s folk-rock (Stephen Stills's "Bluebird"), and '60s rock (Lenny Welch's "Since I Fell for You"). However it was the blues classics that remained her main focus—including Sippie Wallace's "Mighty Tight Woman" and "Woman Be Wise"—both reflecting Bessie Smith–style blues sensibilities of the 1920s.

Bonnie's successive string of albums artfully dodged between traditional blues numbers, recent folk-rock, Motown, and one or two original compositions. She toured constantly and won acclaim and attention in folk-rock circles for her LPs *Give It Up* (1972), *Takin' My Time* (1973), and *Streetlights* (1974). Although she was the darling of the rock critics, none of Bonnie's albums ever reached a higher position than Number 80 on *Billboard's* album chart or sold anywhere near the 500,000 mark that would have certified them gold.

With her 1975 album, *Home Plate,* Bonnie began to leave the traditional blues behind and started aiming toward the mainstream million-selling sound that Linda Ronstadt was enjoying great success with. *Home Plate* was produced by Paul A. Rothchild, who produced Janis Joplin's biggest hits. Rothchild and Raitt enlisted a wonderful who's who of the rock world to play on the album, including Jackson Browne, J. D. Souther, John Sebastian, John Hall (Orleans), Bill Payne (Little Feat), Tom Waits, Emmylou Harris, and Jeff Porcaro (Toto). The album reached Number 43 on the charts and became the new high point in her career.

The next album, *Sweet Forgiveness,* followed the same successful formula, and in 1977 it yielded the hit "Runaway" and was certified gold. For her 1979 album, *The Glow,* Bonnie enlisted Linda Ronstadt's producer, Peter Asher. Again, she found some success, but the album didn't sell as well as *Sweet Forgiveness.*

Meanwhile, the music scene had changed again, and performers like Linda Ronstadt, Carly Simon, and Melanie were all going for hard-edged "new wave" rock sounds. Bonnie followed suit, putting together her own rock band and releasing *Green Light,* which was her stripped-down guitar-rock album.

In the middle of the production for Bonnie's ninth album, *Nine Lives,* Warner Brothers Records rejected several of her tunes, Prince expressed interest in producing for her, and she was experiencing some problems with excessive drinking. For several years she had bought into that whole hard-drinking/fast-living credo that her blues idols had glorified. Finally in 1987 she recognized that she had a problem and enrolled in a program for recovering alcoholics.

Newly sober and approaching her 40th birthday, in 1988 Bonnie was ready to make a fresh start. She felt great, looked wonderful, and was ready to begin all over again. She signed to Capitol Records and commenced work on her "comeback" album, with Don Was as producer. The result was the 1989 hit album *Nick of Time.* Originally the album sold an impressive million copies and then settled down to steady sales. That alone was a significant milestone in her career. However, in February of 1991, Bonnie literally swept through the Grammy Awards and scooped up a record number of five trophies. *Nick of Time* suddenly bolted up to Number One, and proceeded to sell over 5 million copies.

Bonnie's subsequent 1990s albums, *Luck of the Draw* and *Longing in Their Hearts,* have both become multimillion-selling Number One albums, both winning Bonnie additional Grammy Awards. In 1995 Bonnie was featured on the soundtrack album to the film *Boys on the Side,* and it yielded her huge Top 40 hit single version of Roy Orbison's "You Got It." Also in late 1995, Bonnie released her first live album, *Road Tested.*

Aside from her passion about singing, Bonnie's favorite cause is supporting the Rhythm & Blues Foundation. She is the vice chairperson of their corporation and director of the foundation. So many of the rhythm & blues artists of the 1950s and 1960s failed to receive the royalties that are due to them, and Bonnie actively champions the cause of endowing the deserved royalties upon the artists who never received them. She is well known for lending her time and her energy toward worthy causes. In the mid-1990s, Bonnie Raitt is known and respected as the hottest female artist in rock & roll.

Martha & the Vandellas: Martha Reeves, Annette Sterling, Rosalind Ashford *(standing)*

MARTHA REEVES & THE VANDELLAS

ORIGINAL GROUP MEMBERS

Martha Reeves, Annette Sterling, Rosalind Ashford

BIGGEST HITS

- "Come and Get These Memories" (1963)
- "Heat Wave" (1963)
- "Quicksand" (1963)
- "Dancing in the Street" (1964)
- "Wild One" (1964)
- "Nowhere to Run" (1965)
- "You've Been in Love Too Long" (1965)
- "My Baby Loves Me" (1966)
- "I'm Ready for Love" (1966)
- "Jimmy Mack" (1967)
- "Love Bug Leave My Heart Alone" (1967)
- "Honey Chile" (1967)
- "Bless You" (1971)

MARTHA REEVES SOLO HITS

- "The Power of Love" (1974)
- "Wild Night" (1974)
- "Love Blind" (1975)
- "Higher and Higher" (1976)
- "Love Don't Come No Stronger" (1978)
- "Skating in the Streets" (1980)

MILESTONE ALBUMS

- *Come and Get These Memories* (1963)
- *Heat Wave* (1963)
- *Dance Party* (1965)

- *Greatest Hits* (1966)
- *Watchout!* (1967)
- *Martha & the Vandellas Live!* (1967)
- *Ridin' High* (1968)
- *Sugar 'n' Spice* (1969)
- *Natural Resources* (1970)
- *Black Magic* (1972)

BEST MARTHA REEVES SOLO ALBUMS

- *Martha Reeves/Produced by Richard Perry* (1974)
- *The Rest of My Life* (1976)
- *We Meet Again* (1978)
- *The Collection* (1986)

NOTABLE CD PACKAGES

- *Martha Reeves & the Vandellas: Compact Command Performance* [1 CD] (1986)
- *Live Wire: The Singles 1962–1972* [2 CDs] (1993)
- *Martha Reeves & the Vandellas: Motown Milestone* [1 CD] (1995)

GROUP HISTORY

In 1963 and 1964, Martha & the Vandellas was the hottest female singing group in the world. They are one of the most exciting groups to ever come out of the Motown hit-making factory, and their hot string of hits—including "Dancing in the Street," "Heat Wave," "Quicksand," "Nowhere to Run," and "Jimmy Mack"—have made them one of the most beloved groups of the rock era.

Martha Reeves, who possesses a truly exciting and powerful voice, has always been someone who was self-motivated and driven to succeed at whatever she tried. When she was only three years old, Martha and two of her brothers won a singing competition at the church they attended and were awarded a box of chocolate-covered cherries. Ever since that Sunday, Martha had her hopes hung on becoming a singer. It was a goal she never lost sight of, until she attained it.

When she was still in high school in Detroit, she began vocalizing with three local friends: Annette Sterling, Rosalind Ashford, and Gloria Jean Williams. Their first group was called the Del-Phis, and they recorded a single for Checkmate Records, "I'll Let You Know." Meanwhile, all of the girls kept their day jobs. Martha's was at a local dry cleaners. One night following a solo appearance at the Flame Show Bar, Reeves was approached by Motown Records A&R director Mickey Stevenson about coming to an audition. Martha showed up the very next day. A startled Stevenson didn't expect her visit, and after he asked Martha to answer his phone for him, she found herself in a side job as his secretary. Never losing her focus on her singing aspirations, Martha used the secretary job to get her foot in the door at Motown. When Mary Wells failed to show up for a recording session, Martha was whisked in the recording studio to fill in for the missing singer. The "audition" recording led to background session work for Martha, Annette, and Rosalind, and eventually their own turn at stardom as Martha & the Vandellas.

Their second single on Motown-owned Gordy Records, "Come and Get These Memories," cracked the Top 40 Pop charts, and they were suddenly on their way. Late in the summer of 1963, Martha and the Vandellas' "Heat Wave" was released and immediately bolted up to Number One on the R&B charts, and Number Four on the Pop charts. Their follow-up single, "Quicksand," quickly rose to Number Eight on the pop charts, with additional hits "Dancing in the Street" and "Nowhere to Run" not far behind it.

Groomed by Motown's famed elocution teacher, Maxine Powell, Martha & the Vandellas were polished and choreographed, and readied for bookings at posh world-class night spots like the Copacabana in New York City, the Trip in Los Angeles, and the Roostertail in Detroit.

Throughout their ten years at Motown, Martha & the Vandellas released dozens of hit singles, and cemented their place in rock history along the way. During their decade at Motown, Martha found herself adding new Vandellas every few albums. Betty Kelly, Sandra Tilly, and Martha's sister, Lois Reeves, were the recording Vandellas while the act was at Motown. With the 1967 release of their single "Honey Chile," the group changed its name to Martha Reeves & the Vandellas.

After the group's critically acclaimed 1972 album, "Black Magic," it was announced that the group was disbanding and that Martha was going to concentrate on her solo recording career. Her first solo release was the stunning rock/pop/soul classic, *Martha Reeves/Produced by Richard Perry.* Top producer Perry enlisted some of the music world's true A-list musicians to work on Martha's debut solo album, including James Taylor, Billy Preston, Hoyt Axton, and Joe Sample. At the time, the album was famous for being the most expensively produced LP ever released—having cost MCA Records a whopping $250,000. It yielded Martha's compelling version of Van Morrison's "Wild Night," which was later used in the soundtrack of the '90s film *Thelma and Louise.*

Martha continued to record as a solo act on the albums *The Rest of My Life* (1976), *We Meet Again* (1978), *Gotta Keep Moving* (1980), and *Martha Reeves: The Collection* (1987). She kept busy touring internationally as a solo act, and after 1983's Motown reunion television special, "Motown 25," there was renewed interest in Martha reuniting with the Vandellas. She did so, and now tours with either Annette and Rosalind, or her sisters—Lois and Delphine Reeves.

In 1994, Martha Reeves published her memoirs in a book titled *Dancing in the Street: Confessions of a Motown Diva,* which became a big hardcover best-seller. Sadly, Sandra Tilley passed away in 1981 from a brain aneurysm. However, Martha is now close with all five of her remaining Vandellas and insisted that they all be included in the festivities when the group was inducted into the Rock & Roll Hall of Fame in January of 1995. Fittingly, Martha and her original Vandellas were among the star performers to entertain when the Rock & Roll Hall of Fame Museum opened its doors on September 2, 1995.

The Rolling Stones: *(Left to right)* Keith Richards, Ron Wood, Mick Jagger, Charlie Watts, Bill Wyman

THE ROLLING STONES

ORIGINAL GROUP MEMBERS

Mick Jagger, Keith Richards, Bill Wyman, Charlie Watts, Brian Jones (replaced by Mick Taylor, who was replaced by Ron Wood in 1975)

BIGGEST HIT SINGLES

- "Time Is on My Side"' (1964)
- "The Last Time" (1965)
- "(I Can't Get No) Satisfaction" (1965)
- "Get Off of My Cloud" (1965)
- "As Tears Go By" (1965)
- "19th Nervous Breakdown" (1966)
- "Paint It Black" (1966)
- "Mother's Little Helper" (1966)

- "Ruby Tuesday" (1967)
- "Jumping Jack Flash" (1968)
- "Honky Tonk Woman" (1969)
- "Emotional Rescue" (1980)
- "Start Me Up" (1981)
- "Harlem Shuffle" (1986)
- "Mixed Emotions" (1989)
- "High Wire" (1991)
- "Love Is Strong" (1994)
- "Out of Tears" (1994)

MILESTONE ALBUMS

- *Out of Our Heads* (1965)
- *December's Children* (1965)
- *Aftermath* (1966)
- *Between the Buttons* (1967)
- *Flowers* (1967)
- *Their Satanic Majesties Request* (1967)
- *Beggars Banquet* (1968)
- *Let It Bleed* (1969)
- *Sticky Fingers* (1971)
- *Exile on Main Street* (1972)
- *Goats Head Soup* (1974)
- *It's Only Rock & Roll* (1974)
- *Black and Blue* (1976)
- *Some Girls* (1978)
- *Emotional Rescue* (1980)
- *Tattoo You* (1981)
- *Undercover* (1983)
- *Dirty Work* (1986)

- *Steel Wheels* (1989)

- *Flashpoint* (1991)

- *Voodoo Lounge* (1994)

- *Stripped* (1995)

BAND HISTORY

Decidedly sexual, and representing rock & roll at its most raw and seductive, The Rolling Stones in the 1990s are still recording million-selling albums and filling concert arenas around the world. While The Beatles were always those fascinating and lovable lads from Liverpool, The Rolling Stones were always known as the bad boys of rock & roll. While John Lennon was excused his faux pas of equating The Beatles' popularity with Jesus Christ, The Rolling Stones blatantly christened one of their most famous albums *Their Satanic Majesties Request* (1967). When it came to sex and drugs and rock & roll, The Rolling Stones were right in the middle of it.

Mick Jagger met Keith Richards for the first time in school in 1951. They lost contact but rekindled their friendship in 1960, while Jagger was a student at the London School of Economics. The original group-ing of The Rolling Stones first played together on January 14, 1963, at the Flamingo Jazz Club in the Soho district of London. Their debut album, *The Rolling Stones,* was released in 1964, and they became an instant smash in England. The group made its American television debut on the late-night talk show "The Les Crane Show" and were first seen on American prime-time TV on "The Hollywood Palace." When they released their controversial song "Let's Spend the Night Together," Ed Sullivan made them sing it as "Let's Spend *some time* Together," or not appear on his program.

Almost immediately, The Rolling Stones established themselves as one of the most important British rock bands around, second only to The Beatles. Their first string of hits included "Time Is on My Side," "(I Can't Get No) Satisfaction," "Get off of My Cloud," "19th Nervous Breakdown," "Paint It Black," "Mother's Little Helper," "Ruby Tues-day," and "Jumping Jack Flash."

The Rolling Stones were among the first rock stars to be subject to drug busts. In 1967, Mick Jagger, Keith Richards, and Brian Jones were all booked for possession. All three served time in different jails and were released on bail. Later in the year, Jones was again busted. In 1969, Jagger and his girlfriend, Marianne Faithful, were busted together at the London home they shared.

On June 9, 1969, The Rolling Stones replaced Brian Jones with Mick Taylor. On July 3, Brian was found facedown in his swimming pool, drowned. Although it was ruled the simple case of drowning while intoxicated, there have been theories of foul play discussed. However, nothing can be proven, other than the fact that he was inebriated and died.

Another scandal ensued when someone was stabbed to death at The Rolling Stones' famed concert at Altamont on December 6, 1970. The footage from that concert went on to become a famous rock documentary.

When The Beatles broke up in 1970, The Rolling Stones continued onward. Never relinquishing their bad-boy image, the '70s was a very creative decade for The Rolling Stones. They continued to pump out hit after hit, including "Brown Sugar," "Tumbling Dice," "You Can't Always Get What You Want," "Angie," "Fool to Cry," "Miss You," and "Beast of Burden." Mick went on to become a very high profile celebrity, partially due to his transition into movies, notably in the films *Performance* and *Ned Kelly*. In 1975, Ron Wood, from the band The Faces, replaced Mick Taylor. Wood's first album with The Rolling Stones was *Black and Blue*, released in 1976.

Always embroiled in one scandal or another, The Rolling Stones continued to stay in the headlines. In 1976, Keith fell asleep while driving, and crashed his car. When the authorities searched the car, they discovered cocaine and marijuana in it. In January of 1977, Richards was again busted, this time for possession of LSD and cocaine. He and his girlfriend decided to flee for Canada, only to be busted by Canadian police for possession of both cocaine and heroin. He was, however, released on bail in time to perform with the group at the El Mocambo club in Toronto, where the concert album *Love You Live* was recorded.

In 1978 the group released its smash album *Some Girls*, with the huge hit "Miss You." They proved to be as popular as ever. Keith was ultimately forced to undergo treatment for addiction and was sentenced to perform a benefit concert as an act of "community service," to benefit the Canadian National Institute for the Blind. The group swung into the 1980s with their hit album *Emotional Rescue* and the hit title track.

By the mid-'80s the group began splinter off on several solo projects. Jagger released his first solo album, *She's the Boss* (1985), Bill Wyman recorded an album called *Willie and the Poor Boys* (1985), Richards released *Talk Is Cheap* (1988), Ron Wood delved into his artwork, and Charlie Watts played with his own jazz band. They all came back together to record the 1989 album *Steel Wheels,* and to mount the hugely successful concert tour that went along with it.

In 1991 The Rolling Stones released the live album *Flashpoint,* and Mick Jagger appeared in the film *Free Jack* with Emilio Estevez, Anthony Hopkins, and David Johansen. The group's 1994 album, *Voodoo Lounge,* became the first Rolling Stones album without Bill Wyman, who decided to retire from the group. Over 30 years since the release of their debut album, The Rolling Stones don't show any signs that they will be retiring at any time soon. They still sound as raunchy and vital as ever, because—even in their fifties—The Rolling Stones are still rock's reigning bad boys.

Unstoppable—The Rolling Stones recorded a hot new "unplugged"-style album in 1995 called *Stripped.* Recorded in a nightclub in Germany and at several concert rehearsal dates, this new disk showed off the Stones' live charisma without the hollow vastness of stadium concert noise. The album features great acoustic versions of past hits like "Angie" and "Wild Horses," plus an apt cover of Bob Dylan's "Like a Rolling Stone."

The Supremes: Florence Ballard *(standing)*, Mary Wilson, Diana Ross

THE SUPREMES

ORIGINAL GROUP MEMBERS

Mary Wilson, Florence Ballard, Diana Ross

NUMBER ONE HITS

- "Where Did Our Love Go" (1964)
- "Baby Love" (1964)

- "Come See About Me" (1964)
- "Stop! In the Name of Love" (1965)
- "Back in My Arms Again" (1965)
- "I Hear a Symphony" (1965)
- "You Can't Hurry Love" (1966)
- "You Keep Me Hangin' On" (1966)
- "Love Is Here and Now You're Gone" (1967)
- "The Happening" (1967)
- "Love Child" (1968)
- "Someday We'll Be Together" (1969)

BIGGEST '70s HITS

- "Up the Ladder to the Roof" (1970)
- "Stoned Love" (1970)
- "River Deep, Mountain High" [with The Four Tops] (1970)
- "Nathan Jones" (1971)
- "Touch" (1971)
- "Floy Joy" (1972)
- "I'm Gonna Let My Heart Do the Walking" (1976)

MILESTONE ALBUMS

- *Meet the Supremes* (1963)
- *Where Did Our Love Go* (1964)
- *A Bit of Liverpool* (1964)
- *The Supremes Sing Country, Western and Pop* (1965)
- *We Remember Sam Cooke* (1965)
- *More Hits by The Supremes* (1965)
- *Live at the Copa* (1965)
- *I Hear a Symphony* (1966)

- *The Supremes Á Go Go* (1966)
- *The Supremes Sing Holland-Dozier-Holland* (1967)
- *Reflections* (1967)
- *Love Child* (1968)
- *TCB* [with The Temptations] (1968)
- *Let the Sunshine In* (1969)
- *Together* [with The Temptations] (1969)
- *Right On* (1970)
- *New Ways but Love Stays* (1970)
- *The Magnificent Seven* [with The Four Tops] (1970)
- *Touch* (1971)
- *Floy Joy* (1972)
- *High Energy* (1976)

BEST DIANA ROSS SOLO ALBUMS

- *The Boss* (1979)
- *Diana* (1980)

BEST MARY WILSON SOLO ALBUMS

- *Mary Wilson* (1979)
- *Walk the Line* (1991)

NOTABLE CD PACKAGES

- *Anthology* [2 CDs] (1986)
- *The Supremes '70s Greatest Hits and Rare Classics* [1 CD] (1991)

GROUP HISTORY

For most of the 1960s and 1970s, The Supremes were the Number One female singing group in the world. Their unbeatable track record of six back-to-back Number One singles was equalled only by The Beatles, and in the '60s they produced a total of 12 Number One hits, and had one of the most versatile series of hit albums the record business has ever witnessed. They sang Motown Classics (*The Supremes Sing Holland-Dozier-Holland,* 1967), standards (*The Supremes Sing Rodgers and Hart,* 1967), Broadway (*The Supremes Sing and Perform "Funny Girl,"* 1968), exciting R&B (*We Remember Sam Cooke,* 1965), Nashville (*The Supremes Sing Country, Western and Pop,* 1965), British rock (*A Bit of Liverpool,* 1964), contemporary folk (*The Supremes Produced and Arranged by Jimmy Webb,* 1972), and disco (*High Energy,* 1976).

The original trio—Mary Wilson, Florence Ballard, and Diana Ross—lived out a wonderful Cinderella story in the music business. The three girls met while still in high school, and formed their initial group, The Primettes. They won several local Detroit talent contests and became obsessed with the idea of being signed to Berry Gordy Jr.'s fledgling Motown Records. They would hang out at Motown after school each day, hoping for their lucky break. At first it was just participation in background vocals for established artists like Mary Wells, but eventually they were given their own shot at stardom.

From the very start, all three girls took turns singing lead vocals on their records and in their concerts. While looking for a successful formula, the group released a string of 11 unsuccessful singles, including Florence Ballard's exciting "Buttered Popcorn." Finally, in 1964, the group's recording of "Where Did Our Love Go" turned them into an overnight success. With the trio of Eddie Holland, Lamonte Dozier, and Brian Holland writing and producing, Diana's girlish lead vocals, and Mary and Florence's lush background chorus behind her, everything they touched turned to million-selling gold.

Three beautiful black women from the Brewster Projects in Detroit, The Supremes were formally groomed at Motown Records, alongside Marvin Gaye and Martha & the Vandellas. Berry Gordy and Motown Records became famous not only for producing hit records but also for turning local amateur talent into fashionable, exciting, and classy and world-class performers. All three of The Supremes passed with flying colors, and they were the toast of American television screens, appearing with such established performers as Sammy Davis Jr., the Andrews Sisters, Bing Crosby, and Judy Garland. They became the first "rock & roll" act to ever play the prestigious Copacabana nightclub in New York City. They not only triumphed while headlining there, they also recorded the album *The Supremes at the Copa* in 1965.

While The Supremes were to toast of the music world, all wasn't well behind the scenes. On the first series of Supremes albums, both Florence and Mary were given solo songs to sing, and they both performed them in concert. All three girls had strikingly unique personalities. All three Supremes were individually known as distinctively different singing stars, and were treated as equals. However, when Diana began having an affair with Berry Gordy Jr., the group suddenly became a star-making vehicle for her.

In 1967, Florence was suddenly expelled from the group, Cindy Birdsong replaced her, and the trio began using the moniker of "Diana Ross & the Supremes." Following the Number One hit singles "Love Child" and "Someday We'll Be Together," Ross went off on a solo career, and was replaced in the group by Jean Terrell.

Adapting well to changing trends in the music business, Mary, Cindy, and Jean went about creating a whole new list of Supremes classics for the 1970s, including "Up the Ladder to the Roof," "Nathan Jones," and "Stoned Love." In 1973 Lynda Lawrence replaced Cindy, and the group scored a hit with the Stevie Wonder–produced single "Bad Weather." In 1975 Cindy returned to the group, joining Mary Wilson and new Supreme Scherrie Payne. They had a hit with "He's My Man," and Cindy was replaced by Susaye Green. In 1976 the group scored a major disco hit with "I'm Gonna Let My Heart Do the Walking."

Meanwhile, Diana was enjoying a successful solo career, producing hit singles like "I'm Coming Out" and "Ain't No Mountain High Enough." She also stretched out into acting, notably starring in the film *Lady Sings the Blues.*

Unfortunately, Florence's life was startlingly different. When Motown wrote her out of the group, her attempts at a solo career yielded only two single releases. Despondent over her sudden turn of bad luck, she married and started a family, only to end up broke and on welfare. She died in 1976 at the age of 32. Technically, she died of heart failure—but everyone who knew her knew that her death was caused by a broken heart.

After 15 years as "the supreme Supreme," in 1977 Mary Wilson decided that it was time to launch her solo singing career. She has released the albums *Mary Wilson* (1979) and *Walk the Line* (1992). However, her crowning glory came when she wrote her best-selling autobiography *Dreamgirl: My Life as a Supreme* in 1986. The book, which confirmed suspicions of backstage catfights between Ross and Ballard in the 1960s, was heralded as a classic show-business account. Wilson followed it up with her 1990 book, *Supreme Faith: Someday We'll Be Together,* which chronicled the post-Diana Supremes years.

Mary Wilson was one of the stars of a 1995 version of The Motown Revue, which also featured her former label-mates The Temptations, The Four Tops, and Junior Walker & the All Stars. She is also at work on her first novel, *Motor City,* which is about the music business.

Tina Turner

TINA TURNER

BIGGEST HITS

(Ike & Tina Turner releases noted by a *)

- "A Fool in Love" (1960)*
- "I Idolize You" (1960)*
- "It's Gonna Work Out Fine" (1961)*
- "Poor Fool" (1961)
- "Tra La La La" (1962)*
- "You Should'a Treated Me Right" (1962)*
- "I Can't Believe What You Say (for Seeing What You Do)" (1964)*
- "River Deep—Mountain High" (1966)*
- "I've Been Loving You Too Long" (1969)*
- "I'm Gonna Do All I Can (to Do Right By My Man)" (1969)*
- "The Hunter" (1969)*
- "Bold Soul Sister" (1969)*
- "Come Together" (1970)*

- "I Want to Take You Higher" (1970)*
- "Proud Mary" (1971)*
- "Ooh Poo Pah Doo" (1971)*
- "Up in Heh" (1972)*
- "Nutbush City Limits" (1973)*
- "Sexy Ida (Part 1)" (1974)*
- "Baby Get It On" (1975)*
- "Let's Stay Together" (1983)
- "What's Love Got to Do with It?" (1984)
- "Better Be Good to Me" (1984)
- "Private Dancer" (1985)
- "We Don't Need Another Hero" (1985)
- "Out of the Living" (1985)
- "It's Only Love" [with Bryan Adams] (1985)
- "Typical Male" (1986)
- "Two People" (1986)
- "What You See Is What You Get" (1987)
- "The Best" (1989)
- "I Don't Want to Lose You" (1989)
- "Steamy Windows" (1990)
- "Look Me in the Heart" (1990)
- "Be Tender with Me Baby" (1990)
- "It Takes Two" [with Rod Stewart] (1991)
- "Way of the World" (1991)
- "I Don't Really Want to Fight" (1993)
- "Goldeneye" (1995)

MILESTONE ALBUMS

- *Live! The Ike & Tina Turner Show* (1965)*
- *Outta Season* (1969)*
- *In Person* (1969)*

- *River Deep—Mountain High* (1969)*
- *The Hunter* (1969)*
- *Come Together* (1970)*
- *Workin' Together* (1970)*
- *Live at Carnegie Hall/What You Hear Is What You Get* (1971)*
- *'Nuff Said* (1971)*
- *Feel Good* (1972)*
- *Nutbush City Limits* (1973)*
- *Acid Queen* (1975)
- *Private Dancer* (1984)
- *Break Every Rule* (1986)
- *Live in Europe* (1988)
- *Foreign Affair* (1989)
- *What's Love Got to Do with It* [movie soundtrack] (1993)

NOTABLE CD PACKAGES

- *Simply the Best* [1 CD] (1991)
- *Tina: The Collected Recordings* [3 CDs] (1994)

CAREER HISTORY

In 1956, 15-year-old Anna Mae Bullock met band leader Ike Turner in a fairy tale–like fashion. She was with her sister at a club in East St. Louis, Missouri, when Turner's band, The Kings of Rhythm, was playing there. Ike handed the microphone out into the audience to give people a chance to sing with the band. When Ike handed the mike to Anna's sister, Alline, she was too shy to sing in public, so Anna grabbed the mike and leapt to the stage with a frenzy. From that point on, Ike and Anna were inseparable. He talked Anna into adopting the stage name of Tina, and they began one of the most exciting ascensions in rock history.

Promoted as a multifaceted act, with the three back-up singers dubbed The Ikettes, The Ike & Tina Turner Revue began its rock legacy with the 1960 hit, "A Fool in Love." In the early '60s, The Ike & Tina Turner Revue racked up several hits, including "It's Gonna Work Out Fine," "Poor Fool," and "I Can't Believe What You Say (for Seeing What You Do)." In 1966 Ike and Tina became acquainted with master producer Phil Spector, and Phil signed the act to a production deal. The resulting masterpiece was the album *River Deep—Mountain High*, which produced the title hit.

On the 1970 albums *Come Together* and *Workin' Together*, Ike and Tina began recording hot new cover versions of current rock & roll classics. They recorded The Rolling Stones' "Honky Tonk Woman," as well as The Beatles' "Come Together" and Sly & the Family Stone's "I Want To Take You Higher." However, the high point came on their dramatic version of Creedence Clearwater Revival's "Proud Mary." The song became the group's biggest hit. In 1973, a song that Tina wrote, "Nutbush City Limits," became another signature number for Ike & Tina Turner.

When it came time to film an all-star screen version of The Who's fabled rock opera, *Tommy*, Tina was selected for the role of the Acid Queen, singing the song of the same name on the film's soundtrack album. Tina's trademark skimpy outfits and frenzied stage dancing worked perfectly with the flamboyant role, and she drew rave reviews for her appearance. Her film debut prompted her first solo album, *Acid Queen*, on which she also sang her versions of The Rolling Stones' "Under My Thumb" and "Let's Spend the Night Together," The Who's "I Can See for Miles," and Led Zeppelin's "Whole Lotta Love."

Meanwhile, what Tina's adoring public didn't know was that while all of this was going on, Ike was abusing substances and physically abusing Tina. In 1976 she walked out on Ike, and turned her back on any money that should have rightfully been hers. She looked within herself and into her newly adopted Buddhist faith for strength over the next couple of years. In 1979 she met an Australian promoter named Roger Davies, and she signed with him as her manager. She was without a record label at the time, so securing one became a main priority. Davies began to plot a high-profile course for Tina, to get her back in the public eye.

Several of her friends in show business lent her a helping hand. In 1981, Tina toured as The Rolling Stones' opening act, and she made a high-profile guest appearance on a Rod Stewart satellite-broadcast TV concert special. On it she was seen singing a trio version of the song "Stay with Me" with Stewart and Kim Carnes. Not long afterward, the London-based group Haircut 100 invited her to record a new version of The Temptations' song "Ball of Confusion." She turned in a bravura performance. Next, her friend David Bowie brought several EMI Record executives to attend one of her performances at the Ritz in New York City, in hopes that they would sign her to a deal. She ended up with a contract from Capitol Records, and in December of 1983, her version of Al Green's "Let's Stay Together" put her back on the charts.

In 1984 she toured as Lionel Richie's opening act, and recorded the comeback album of a lifetime, *Private Dancer*. Released mid-year, it remained in the Top Ten for ten consecutive months, selling more than 10 million copies worldwide. She swept to the top of the charts with her phenomenal Number One hit "What's Love Got to Do with It?" and the sassy video that went along with it. Tina looked and sounded fantastic, and she was suddenly getting all of the attention and all of the acclaim that was due to her. In February of 1985 Tina won three Grammy Awards, for her hits "What's Love Got to Do with It?" and "Better Be Good to Me."

Continuing along her comeback trail, Tina co-starred in the Mel Gibson film *Mad Max, Beyond Thunderdome*, as villainess Auntie Entity. She sang two songs on the movie soundtrack—"We Don't Need Another Hero" and "One of the Living"—both of which became huge chart hits. In June of 1986 Tina appeared with Eric Clapton, Bryan Adams, and Elton John at a charity event, the Prince's Trust, in London, before Prince Charles and Princess Diana of England.

On August 28, 1986, Tina received a star on the Hollywood Boulevard "Walk of Fame," just outside of the famed Capitol Records building. That same year she released her next album, *Break Every Rule*, which included the Number One hit "Typical Male," and additional hits "Two People" and "What You Get Is What You See."

Tina embarked on an extensive concert tour, which provided the tracks for her exciting 1988 double album, *Live in Europe*. Along the way, she broke box-office records in 13 European countries. The album went on to win her still another Grammy Award.

In contrast, while Tina was the toast of Europe and America, Ike Turner was busted for cocaine possession and began serving a four-year jail sentence in July of 1989.

That fall, Tina released her critically acclaimed *Foreign Affair* album. It provided her with further hits, "The Best," "Steamy Windows," and "Look Me in the Heart." On June 28, 1990, Tina Turner became the first 20th-century female peformer to play a concert at the Palace of Versailles, outside of Paris. In 1991, she and Ike were inducted into the Rock & Roll Hall of Fame.

In 1993, the movie version of Tina's compelling autobiography, *I, Tina,* was released as *What's Love Got to Do With It.* The film featured Angela Bassett as Tina and Laurence Fishburn as Ike, and both performers received Academy Award nominations for their dramatic portrayals. Tina provided all of her own newly recorded vocals for Bassett to dub in the soundtrack and ended up with another best-selling album, as well as the sizzling new hit, "I Don't Wanna Fight."

In 1994, the three-CD boxed set, *Tina: The Collected Recordings,* was released, as another milestone to the hardest working woman in rock & roll. The following year, Tina sang the theme song for the 1995 James Bond film, *Goldeneye.* In recent years Tina has moved to Cologne, Germany, where she spends much of her time. In Europe they know how to treat royalty correctly—rock & roll's queen, Tina Turner, rightfully feels at home there!

Birth Dates of Rock Stars

JANUARY 1

Country Joe McDonald / 1942 (Country Joe & the Fish)

Grandmaster Flash / 1958 ("White Lines [Don't Do It]")

JANUARY 2

Chick Churchill / 1949 (Ten Years After)

Roger Miller / 1936 ("King of the Road")

George Martin / 1926 (producer of all of The Beatles'
albums)

JANUARY 3

Stephen Stills / 1945 (Buffalo Springfield/Crosby, Stills
& Nash)

JANUARY 4

John McLaughlin / 1942 (Mahavishnu Orchestra)

JANUARY 5

Chris Stein / 1950 (Blondie)

Sam Phillips / 1923 (president of legendary Sun Records)

George Brown / 1949 (Kool & the Gang)

Bryan Hitt / 1954 (REO Speedwagon)

JANUARY 6

Wilbert Harrison / 1929 ("Kansas City")

Sandy Denny / 1947 (Fairport Convention)

Malcolm Young / 1953 (AC/DC)

Mark O'Toole / 1964 (Frankie Goes to Hollywood)

Syd Barrett / 1945 (Pink Floyd)

Kenny Loggins—January 7

JANUARY 7

Kenny Loggins / 1948 (Loggins & Messina)

Paul Revere / 1942 (Paul Revere & the Raiders)

JANUARY 8

Elvis Presley / 1935 ("Teddy Bear")

David Bowie / 1947 ("Young American")

Robbie Krieger / 1946 (The Doors)

Little Anthony / 1941 (Little Anthony & the Imperials)

Mike Reno / 1955 (Loverboy)

Terry Sylvester / 1945 (replaced Graham Nash in the Hollies)

JANUARY 9

Joan Baez / 1941 ("The Night They Drove Old Dixie Down")

Jimmy Page / 1944 (Led Zeppelin)

Scott Engel / 1944 (The Walker Brothers)

JANUARY 10

Rod Stewart / 1945 ("Maggie May")

Pat Benatar / 1953 ("Love Is a Battlefield")

Jim Croce / 1943 ("Bad, Bad Leroy Brown")

Jerry Wexler / 1917 (producer of Aretha Franklin's '60s and '70s hits)

Donald Fagen / 1948 (Steely Dan)

Johnny Ray / 1927 ("Cry")

JANUARY 11

Vicki Peterson / 1960 (The Bangles)

Slim Harpo / 1924 ("Rainin' in My Heart")

JANUARY 12

Long John Baldry / 1941 ("Don't Try to Lay No Boogie-Woogie on the King of Rock & Roll")

Cynthia Robinson / 1946 (Sly & the Family Stone)

JANUARY 13

Cornelius Bumpus / 1952 (Moby Grape/The Doobie Brothers)

Graham "Suggs" McPherson / 1961 (Madness)

JANUARY 14

Carl Chas Smash Smyth / 1959 (Madness)

Allen Toussaint / 1938 (writer "Lady Marmalade")

Tim Harris / 1948 (The Foundations)

JANUARY 15

Captain Beefheart / 1941 (Captain Beefheart & His Magic Band)

Martha Davis / 1951 (The Motels)

JANUARY 16

Sade Adu / 1959 ("Smooth Operator")

Bob Bogle / 1937 (The Ventures)

JANUARY 17

Bobby "Blue" Bland / 1930 ("Ain't Nothing You Can Do")

Paul Young / 1956 ("Every Time You Go Away")

Chris Montez / 1944 ("Call Me")

William Hart / 1945 (The Delphonics)

Mick Taylor / 1948 (The Rolling Stones)

JANUARY 18

David Ruffin / 1941 (The Temptations)

Tom Bailey / 1956 (The Thompson Twins)

JANUARY 19

Janis Joplin / 1943 ("Me and Bobby McGee")

Robert Palmer / 1949 ("Addicted to Love")

Phil Everly / 1939 (The Everly Brothers)

Dewey Bunnell / 1952 (America)

JANUARY 20

Ron Townson / 1933 (The Fifth Dimension)

Eric Stewart / 1945 (Wayne Fontana & the Mindbenders/10cc)

Paul Stanley / 1950 (KISS)

Leadbelly / 1889 (rock pioneer/"Rock Island Line")

JANUARY 21

Richie Havens / 1941 ("Here Comes the Sun")

Billy Ocean / 1950 ("Get Out of My Dreams [and into My Car]")

Edwin Starr / 1942 ("War")

Jimmy Ibbotson / 1947 (The Nitty Gritty Dirt Band)

JANUARY 22

Sam Cooke / 1935 ("You Send Me")

Micki Harris / 1940 (The Shirelles)

Steve Perry / 1953 (Journey)

JANUARY 23

Anita Pointer / 1948 (The Pointer Sisters)

Pat Simmons / 1950 (The Doobie Brothers)

Robin Zander / 1953 (Cheap Trick)

Bill Cunningham / 1950 (The Box Tops)

Jerry Lawson / 1944 (The Persuasions)

JANUARY 24

Warren Zevon / 1947 ("Werewolves of London")

Neil Diamond / 1941 ("Brother Love's Travelling Salvation Show)

JANUARY 25

Richard Finch / 1954 (K.C. & the Sunshine Band)

Malcolm Green / 1953 (Split Enz)

Joe Strummer / 1955 (The Clash)

Andy Cox / 1956 (The Beat)

JANUARY 26

Eddie Van Halen / 1957 (Van Halen)

Jazzie B. / 1963 (Soul II Soul)

David Briggs / 1951 (Little River Band)

JANUARY 27

Nick Mason / 1945 (Pink Floyd)

Nedra Tilley / 1946 (The Ronettes)

Brian Downey / 1951 (Thin Lizzy)

Seth Justman / 1951 (The J. Geils Band)

Elmore James / 1918 (blues guitar pioneer)

JANUARY 28

Rick Allen / 1946 (The Box Tops)

Corky Laing / 1948 (Mountain)

Brian Keenan / 1944 (The Chambers Brothers)

Dick Taylor / 1943 (The Pretty Things)

JANUARY 29

David Byron / 1947 (Uriah Heep)

Tommy Ramone / 1949 (The Ramones)

Roddy Frame / 1964 (Aztec Camera)

JANUARY 30

Steve Marriott / 1947 (Humble Pie)

Marty Balin / 1942 (Jefferson Airplane/Starship)

Jody Watley / 1959 ("Looking for a New Love")

Joe Terranova / 1941 (Danny & the Juniors)

JANUARY 31

Phil Collins / 1951 (Genesis)

Henry Wayne Casey / 1951 (K.C. & the Sunshine Band)

Phil Manzanera / 1951 (Roxy Music)

John Lydon / 1956 (Public Image Ltd.)

Terry Kath / 1946 (Chicago)

FEBRUARY 1

Don Everly / 1937 (The Everly Brothers)

Ray Sawyer / 1939 (Dr. Hook & the Medicine Show)

Rick James / 1952 ("Super Freak")

Mike Campbell / 1954 (Tom Petty & the Heartbreakers)

FEBRUARY 2

Graham Nash / 1942 (The Hollies/Crosby, Stills & Nash)

Peter Lucia / 1947 (Tommy James & the Shondells)

Ross Valory / 1949 (Journey)

FEBRUARY 3

Melanie / 1947 ("Candles in the Rain")

Dave Davies / 1947 (The Kinks)

Eric Haydock / 1943 (The Hollies)

Angelo D'Aleo / 1941 (Dion & the Belmonts)

Johnny "Guitar" Watson / 1935 ("A Real Mother for Ya")

Dennis Edwards / 1943 (replaced David Ruffin in The Temptations)

FEBRUARY 4

Alice Cooper / 1948 ("I'm Eighteen")

Florence LaRue / 1944 (The Fifth Dimension)

Jerry Shirley / 1952 (Humble Pie)

John Steel / 1941 (The Animals)

FEBRUARY 5

Cory Wells / 1944 (Three Dog Night)

Bobby Brown / 1969 ("My Prerogative")

Al Kooper / 1944 (Blood, Sweat & Tears)

David Denny / 1948 (The Steve Miller Band)

FEBRUARY 6

Bob Marley / 1945 ("Roots Rock Reggae")

Rick Astley / 1966 ("Never Gonna Give You Up")

Natalie Cole / 1950 ("Pink Cadillac")

Fabian / 1943 ("Turn Me Loose")

FEBRUARY 7

Jimmy Greenspoon / 1948 (Three Dog Night)

David Bryan / 1962 (Bon Jovi)

Alan Lancaster / 1949 (Status Quo)

Steve Bronski / 1960 (Bronski Beat)

FEBRUARY 8

Vince Neil / 1961 (Mötley Crüe)

Creed Bratton / 1943 (The Grass Roots)

Tom Rush / 1941 ("Urge for Going")

FEBRUARY 9

Carole King / 1941 ("I Feel the Earth Move")

Dennis "Dee Tee" Thomas / 1951 (Kool & the Gang)

FEBRUARY 10

Roberta Flack / 1939 ("Killing Me Softly with His Song")

Peter Allen / 1944 ("Fly Away")

Jimmy Merchant / 1940 (Frankie Lyman & the Teenagers)

Don Wilson / 1937 (The Ventures)

FEBRUARY 11

Gene Vincent / 1935 ("Be-Bop-A-Lula")

Gerry Goffin / 1939 (songwriter with Carole King: "Up on the Roof")

FEBRUARY 12

Ray Manzarek / 1943 (The Doors)

Joe Schermie / 1945 (Three Dog Night)

Steve Hackett / 1950 (Genesis)

FEBRUARY 13

Peter Tork / 1942 (The Monkees)

Tony Butler / 1947 (Big Country)

Ed Gagliardi / 1952 (Foreigner)

Mark Fox / 1958 (Haircut 100)

Peter Hook / 1956 (New Order)

FEBRUARY 14

Tim Buckley / 1947 ("Morning Glory")

Eric Anderson / 1943 (songwriter: "Thirsty Boots")

FEBRUARY 15

Melissa Manchester / 1951 ("Don't Cry Out Loud")

Mick Avory / 1944 (The Kinks)

Mikey Craig / 1960 (Culture Club)

Brian Holland / 1941 (one third of Motown producing/songwriting trio Holland/Dozier/Holland)

FEBRUARY 16

Sonny Bono / 1935 (Sonny & Cher)

Andy Taylor / 1961 (Duran Duran)

FEBRUARY 17

Gene Pitney / 1941 ("Town Without Pity")

Bobby Lewis / 1933 ("Tossin' and Turnin'")

FEBRUARY 18

Yoko Ono / 1933 ("Walking on Thin Ice")

Robbie Bachman / 1953 (Bachman-Turner Overdrive)

Herman Santiago / 1941 (Frankie Lyman & the Teenagers)

Dennis DeYoung / 1947 (STYX)

FEBRUARY 19

Smokey Robinson / 1940 ("Cruisin' ")

Lou Christie / 1943 ("Lightnin' Strikes")

Tony Lommi / 1948 (Black Sabbath)

Falco / 1957 ("Rock Me Amadeus")

FEBRUARY 20

J. Geils / 1946 (The J. Geils Band)

Randy California / 1951 (Spirit)

Walter Becker / 1950 (Steely Dan)

Barbara Ellis / 1940 (The Fleetwoods)

Jimmy Yancey / 1898 (boogie piano pioneer)

FEBRUARY 21

Jerry Harrison / 1949 (Talking Heads)

Ranking Roger / 1961 (General Public/The Beat)

FEBRUARY 22

Bobby Hendricks / 1938 (The Drifters)

Michael Wilton / 1962 (Queensryche)

FEBRUARY 23

Johnny Winter / 1944 ("Jumpin' Jack Flash")

Brad Whitford / 1952 (Aerosmith)

Howard Jones / 1955 ("No One Is to Blame")

Rusty Young / 1946 (Poco)

FEBRUARY 24

Paul Jones / 1942 (Manfred Mann)

Lonnie Turner / 1947 (The Steve Miller Band)

Nicky Hopkins / 1944 (recording session piano player)

FEBRUARY 25

George Harrison / 1943 (The Beatles)

Stuart "Woody" Wood / 1957 (The Bay City Rollers)

FEBRUARY 26

Fats Domino / 1928 ("Blueberry Hill")

Jonathan Cain / 1950 (Journey)

Mitch Ryder / 1945 (Mitch Ryder & the Detroit Wheels)

Bob "The Bear" Hite / 1943 (Canned Heat)

Johnny Cash / 1932 ("Ring of Fire")

FEBRUARY 27

Neal Schon / 1954 (Journey)

Eddie Gray / 1948 (Tommy James & the Shondells)

Paul Humphreys / 1960 (Orchestral Maneuvers in the Dark)

Adrian Smith / 1957 (Iron Maiden)

FEBRUARY 28

Cindy Wilson / 1957 (The B-52's)

Brian Jones / 1942 (The Rolling Stones)

Ronnie Rosman / 1945 (Tommy James & the Shondells)

Joe South / 1940 ("Games People Play")

FEBRUARY 29

Gretchen Christopher / 1940 (The Fleetwoods)

MARCH 1

Roger Daltrey / 1945 (The Who)

Mike D'Abo / 1944 (Manfred Mann)

Harry Belefonte / 1927 (participant in "We Are the World")

MARCH 2

Lou Reed / 1943 ("Walk on the Wild Side")

Eddie Money / 1949 ("Take Me Home Tonight")

Dale Bozzio / 1955 (Missing Persons)

Jon Bon Jovi / 1962 (Bon Jovi)

MARCH 3

Willie Chambers / 1938 (The Chambers Brothers)

Mike Pender / 1942 (The Searchers)

Dave Amato / 1953 (REO Speedwagon)

Junior Parker / 1927 (songwriter: "Mystery Train")

MARCH 4

Chris Squire / 1948 (Yes)

Bobby Womack / 1944 ("Lookin' for a Love")

Emilio Estefan / 1953 (Miami Sound Machine)

Chris Rea / 1951 ("Fool [If You Think It's Over]")

MARCH 5

Andy Gibb / 1958 ("Shadow Dancing")

Eddie Grant / 1948 ("Electric Avenue")

Alan Clark / 1952 (Dire Straits)

MARCH 6

Mary Wilson / 1944 (The Supremes)

David Gilmour / 1944 (Pink Floyd)

Kiki Dee / 1947 ("I Got the Music in Me")

Hugh Grundy / 1945 (The Zombies)

MARCH 7

Peter Wolf / 1946 (The J. Geils Band)

Chris White / 1943 (The Zombies)

Peggy March / 1948 ("I Will Follow Him")

MARCH 8

Micky Dolenz / 1945 (The Monkees)

Randy Meisner / 1946 (The Eagles)

Peter Gill / 1964 (Frankie Goes to Hollywood)

Gary Numan / 1958 ("Cars")

MARCH 9

Mark Lindsay / 1942 (Paul Revere & the Raiders)

Robin Trower / 1945 (Procol Harum)

Lloyd Price / 1933 ("Personality")

Jeffrey Osborne / 1948 ("On the Wings of Love")

Jimmy Fadden / 1948 (The Nitty Gritty Dirt Band)

James Taylor—March 12

MARCH 10

Dean Torrence / 1940 (Jan & Dean)

Tom Scholz / 1947 (Boston)

MARCH 11

Mark Stein / 1945 (Vanilla Fudge)

Bobby McFerrin / 1950 ("Don't Worry Be Happy")

Bruce Watson / 1961 (Big Country)

Ric Rothwell / 1944 (Wayne Fontana & the Mindbenders)

MARCH 12

James Taylor / 1948 ("Fire and Rain")

Paul Kantner / 1942 (Jefferson Airplane/Starship)

Steve Harris / 1957 (Iron Maiden)

Bill Payne / 1949 (Little Feat)

MARCH 13

Neil Sedaka / 1939 ("Breaking Up Is Hard to Do")

Adam Clayton / 1960 (U2)

Ronnie Rogers / 1959 (T' Pau)

MARCH 14

Quincy Jones / 1933 (producer/performer: "Stuff Like That")

David Byrne / 1952 (Talking Heads)

Jim Pons / 1943 (The Turtles)

MARCH 15

Sly Stone / 1944 (Sly & the Family Stone)

Dee Snyder / 1955 (Twisted Sister)

Mike Love / 1941 (The Beach Boys)

Terence Trent D'Arby / 1962 ("Wishing Well")

MARCH 16

Nancy Wilson / 1954 (Heart)

Jerry Jeff Walker / 1942 (songwriter: "Mr. Bojangles")

MARCH 17

John Sebastian / 1944 (The Lovin' Spoonful)

Vito Picone / 1940 (The Elegants)

Scott Gorham / 1951 (Thin Lizzy)

Wally Stocker / 1954 (The Babys)

Harold Brown / 1946 (War)

MARCH 18

Irene Cara / 1959 ("Fame")

Wilson Pickett / 1941 ("In the Midnight Hour")

John Hartman / 1950 (The Doobie Brothers)

Barry Wilson / 1947 (Procol Harum)

MARCH 19

Ricky Wilson / 1953 (The B-52's)

Paul Atkinson / 1946 (The Zombies)

MARCH 20

Jimmie Vaughan / 1951 (The Fabulous Thunderbirds)

Slim Jim Phantom / 1961 (Stray Cats)

Carl Palmer / 1947 (Emerson, Lake & Palmer)

MARCH 21

Rosemary Stone / 1945 (Sly & the Family Stone)

Roger Hodgson / 1950 (Supertramp)

MARCH 22

Stephanie Mills / 1957 ("Never Knew Love Like This Before")

Jeremy Clyde / 1944 (Chad & Jeremy)

George Benson / 1943 ("Give Me the Night")

Patrick Olive / 1947 (Hot Chocolate)

MARCH 23

Chaka Khan / 1953 ("I'm Every Woman")

Marti Pellow / 1966 (Wet Wet Wet)

MARCH 24

Nick Lowe / 1949 ("Cruel to Be Kind")

Lee Oskar / 1946 (War)

MARCH 25

Aretha Franklin / 1942 ("Freeway of Love")

Elton John / 1947 ("Your Song")

MARCH 26

Steven Tyler / 1948 (Aerosmith)

Diana Ross / 1944 (The Supremes)

Teddy Pendergrass / 1950 ("Turn Out the Lights")

Fred Parris / 1936 (The Five Satins)

Fran Sheehan / 1949 (Boston)

MARCH 27

Tony Banks / 1951 (Genesis)

Billy Mackenzie / 1957 (The Associates)

Clark Datchler / 1961 (Johnny Hates Jazz)

MARCH 28

John Evan / 1948 (Jethro Tull)

Johnny Burnette / 1934 ("You're Sixteen")

Chuck Portz / 1945 (The Turtles)

MARCH 29

Bobby Kimball / 1947 (Toto)

Vangelis / 1943 ("Chariots of Fire")

MARCH 30

Eric Clapton / 1945 ("Tears in Heaven")

M.C. Hammer / 1962 ("U Can't Touch This")

Graeme Edge / 1944 (The Moody Blues)

Jim Dandy Mangrum / 1948 (Black Oak Arkansas)

Randy Vanwarmer / 1955 ("Just When I Needed You Most")

MARCH 31

Herb Alpert / 1935 (Herb Alpert & the Tijuana Brass)

Angus Young / 1959 (AC/DC)

Sean Hopper / 1953 (Huey Lewis & the News)

Tony Brock / 1954 (The Babys)

APRIL 1

Rudolph Isley / 1939 (The Isley Brothers)

Jeff Porcaro / 1954 (Toto)

John Barbata / 1946 (The Turtles)

Billy Currie / 1952 (Ultravox)

APRIL 2

Marvin Gaye / 1939 ("Can I Get a Witness")

Leon Russell / 1941 ("Tight Rope")

APRIL 3

Tony Orlando / 1944 (Tony Orlando & Dawn)

Jan Berry / 1941 (Jan & Dean)

Mel Schacher / 1951 (Grand Funk Railroad)

Richard Manuel / 1945 (The Band)

APRIL 4

Major Lance / 1941 ("The Monkey")

Mick Mars / 1955 (Motley Crüe)

Dave Hill / 1952 (Slade)

Muddy Waters / 1915 (pioneer: "Rollin' Stone")

APRIL 5

Agnetha Faltskog / 1950 (ABBA)

Ronnie White / 1939 (Smokey Robinson & the Miracles)

Tony Williams / 1928 (The Platters)

David LaFlame / 1941 (It's a Beautiful Day)

APRIL 6

Ralph Cooper / 1951 (Air Supply)

Tony Connor / 1947 (Hot Chocolate)

John Stax / 1944 (The Pretty Things)

APRIL 7

Mick Abrahams / 1943 (Jethro Tull)

Bill Kreutzmann / 1946 (The Grateful Dead)

Bruce Gary / 1952 (The Knack)

APRIL 8

Julian Lennon / 1963 ("Too Late for Goodbyes")

Steve Howe / 1947 (Yes/Asia)

APRIL 9

Carl Perkins / 1932 ("Blue Suede Shoes")

Mark Kelly / 1961 (Marillion)

APRIL 10

Brian Setzer / 1960 (Stray Cats)

Bunny Wailer / 1947 (Bob Marley & the Wailers)

APRIL 11

Stuart Adamson / 1958 (Big Country)

Delroy Pearson / 1970 (Five Star)

APRIL 12

John Kay / 1944 (Steppenwolf)

David Cassidy / 1950 ("Cherish")

Lois Reeves / 1948 (Martha Reeves & the Vandellas)

Will Sergeant / 1958 (Echo & the Bunnymen)

Herbie Hancock / 1940 ("Rockit")

APRIL 13

Al Green / 1946 ("Let's Stay Together")

Jack Casady / 1944 (Jefferson Airplane/Hot Tuna)

Lowell George / 1945 (Little Feat)

Lester Chambers / 1940 (The Chambers Brothers)

APRIL 14

Ritchie Blackmore / 1945 (Deep Purple/Ritchie Blackmore's Rainbow)

Buddy Knox / 1933 ("Party Doll")

Larry Ferguson / 1948 (Hot Chocolate)

APRIL 15

Dave Edmunds / 1944 ("I Hear You Knocking")

Tony Williams / 1928 (The Platters)

Bessie Smith / 1894 (blues pioneer: "Empty Bed Blues")

Phil Lesh / 1940 (The Grateful Dead)

Graeme Clark / 1966 (Wet Wet Wet)

APRIL 16

Dusty Springfield / 1939 ("You Don't Have to Say You Love Me")

Bobby Vinton / 1935 ("Blue Velvet")

Gerry Rafferty / 1947 ("Baker Street")

APRIL 17

John Oates / 1949 (Hall & Oates)

Bill Kreutzmann / 1946 (The Grateful Dead)

APRIL 18

Skip Spence / 1946 (Moby Grape)

Les Pattinson / 1958 (Echo & the Bunnymen)

Mike Vickers / 1941 (Manfred Mann)

APRIL 19

Alan Price / 1941 (The Animals)

Mark Volman / 1947 (The Turtles)

APRIL 20

Luther Vandross / 1951 ("Never Too Much")

Craig Frost / 1948 (Grand Funk Railroad)

Jimmy Winston / 1945 (The Small Faces)

APRIL 21

Iggy Pop / 1947 ("Real Wild Child")

Paul Davis / 1948 ("I Go Crazy")

Robert Smith / 1959 (The Cure)

APRIL 22

Peter Frampton / 1950 ("Baby, I Love Your Way")

Ace Frehley / 1951 (KISS)

Glen Campbell / 1938 ("By the Time I Get to Phoenix")

Craig Logan / 1969 (Bros)

APRIL 23

Roy Orbison / 1936 ("In Dreams")

Steve Clark / 1960 (Def Leppard)

APRIL 24

Barbra Streisand / 1942 ("Stony End")

Doug "Cosmo" Clifford / 1945 (Creedence Clearwater Revival)

Glenn Cornick / 1947 (Jethro Tull)

APRIL 25

Bjorn Ulvaeus / 1945 (ABBA)

Stu Cook / 1945 (Creedence Clearwater Revival)

Peter Frampton—April 22

Michael Brown / 1949 (The Left Banke)

Fish / 1958 (Marillion)

Albert King / 1923 (pioneer: "Born Under a Bad Sign")

APRIL 26

Bobby Rydell / 1942 ("Volare")

Roger Taylor / 1960 (Duran Duran)

Ma Rainey / 1886 (blues pioneer)

APRIL 27

Kate Pierson / 1948 (The B-52's)

Pete Ham / 1947 (Badfinger)

Sheena Easton / 1959 ("For Your Eyes Only")

APRIL 28

Duane Eddy / 1938 ("Peter Gunn")

Eddie Jobson / 1955 (Roxy Music)

APRIL 29

Tommy James / 1947 (Tommy James & the Shondells)

Carl Gardner / 1928 (The Coasters)

Klaus Voorman / 1942 (Manfred Mann)

Francis Rossi / 1949 (Status Quo)

APRIL 30

Bobby Vee / 1943 ("Devil or Angel")

Merril Osmond / 1953 (The Osmonds)

Johnny Horton / 1927 ("The Battle of New Orleans")

Willie Nelson / 1933 ("On the Road Again")

MAY 1

Rita Coolidge / 1944 ("We're All Alone")

Judy Collins / 1939 ("Both Sides Now")

Ray Parker Jr. / 1954 ("Ghostbusters")

Tony Ashton / 1946 (Family)

Phil Smith / 1959 (Haircut 100)

Rita Coolidge—May 1

MAY 2

Lesley Gore / 1946 ("It's My Party")

Lou Gramm / 1950 (Foreigner)

Prescott Niles / 1954 (The Knack)

Goldy McJohn / 1945 (Steppenwolf)

Link Wray / 1935 ("Rawhide")

May 3

James Brown / 1928 ("I Got You [I Feel Good]")

Frankie Valli / 1937 (The Four Seasons)

Christopher Cross / 1951 ("Sailing")

Mary Hopkin / 1950 ("Those Were the Days")

Pete Seeger / 1919 ("Little Boxes")

May 4

Nicholas Ashford / 1943 (Ashford & Simpson)

Ed Cassidy / 1931 (Spirit)

Ronnie Bond / 1943 (The Troggs)

Jackie Jackson / 1951 (The Jackson Five)

May 5

Johnnie Taylor / 1938 ("Who's Makin' Love")

Frank Esler-Smith / 1948 (Air Supply)

Ian McCulloch / 1959 (Echo & the Bunnymen)

May 6

Bob Seger / 1945 ("Night Moves")

Larry Steinbachek / 1960 (Bronski Beat)

Herbie Cox / 1939 (The Cleftones)

May 7

Johnny Maestro / 1939 (The Brooklyn Bridge/The Crests)

Jimmy Ruffin / 1939 ("What Becomes of the Brokenhearted")

Rick West / 1943 (The Tremeloes)

Prairie Prince / 1950 (Journey)

MAY 8

Toni Tennille / 1943 (The Captain & Tennille)

Ricky Nelson / 1940 ("Travelin' Man")

Alex Van Halen / 1955 (Van Halen)

Chris Frantz / 1951 (Talking Heads)

John Fred / 1941 (John Fred & His Playboy Band)

Paul Samwell-Smith / 1943 (The Yardbirds)

MAY 9

Billy Joel / 1949 ("Piano Man")

Tommy Roe / 1943 ("Sweet Pea")

Dave Prater / 1937 (Sam & Dave)

Richie Furay / 1944 (Buffalo Springfield/Poco)

Steve Katz / 1945 (Blood, Sweat & Tears)

MAY 10

Bono / 1960 (U2)

Dave Mason / 1947 (Traffic)

Donovan Leitch / 1946 ("Mellow Yellow")

Danny Rapp / 1941 (Danny & the Juniors)

MAY 11

Eric Burden / 1941 (The Animals)

Les Chadwick / 1943 (Gerry & the Pacemakers)

MAY 12

Steve Winwood / 1948 (Traffic/Spencer Davis Group)

Ian Dury / 1942 (The Blockheads)

David Walker / 1943 (Gary Lewis & the Playboys)

Ian McLagan / 1945 (The Small Faces)

MAY 13

Stevie Wonder / 1950 ("Superstition")

Mary Wells / 1943 ("My Guy")

Peter Gabriel / 1950 (Genesis)

Ritchie Valens / 1941 ("La Bamba")

Magic Dick / 1945 (The J. Geils Band)

MAY 14

Bobby Darin / 1936 ("Splish Splash")

Jack Bruce / 1943 (Cream)

Danny Wood / 1969 (New Kids on the Block)

Fab Morvan / 1966 (Milli Vanilli)

MAY 15

Brian Eno / 1948 (Roxy Music)

Mike Oldfield / 1953 ("Tubular Bells")

Graham Goble / 1947 (The Little River Band)

MAY 16

Janet Jackson / 1966 ("What Have You Done for Me Lately?")

Jimmy Osmond / 1963 (The Osmonds)

Glenn Gregory / 1958 (Heaven 17)

Barbara Lee / 1947 (The Chiffons)

Billy Cobham / 1944 (session drummer)

MAY 17

Bill Bruford / 1948 (Yes)

Paul Di'anno / 1959 (Iron Maiden)

Jordan Knight / 1970 (New Kids on the Block)

MAY 18

Rick Wakeman / 1949 (Yes)

William Wallace / 1949 (The Guess Who)

MAY 19

Grace Jones / 1952 ("I Need a Man")

Dusty Hill / 1949 (ZZ Top)

Joey Ramone / 1952 (The Ramones)

Phillip Rudd / 1946 (AC/DC)

Pete Townshend / 1945 (The Who)

MAY 20

Cher / 1946 ("Gypsies, Tramps and Theives")

Joe Cocker / 1944 ("With a Little Help from My Friends")

Brian Nash / 1963 (Frankie Goes to Hollywood)

Nick Heyward / 1961 (Haircut 100)

MAY 21

Ronald Isley / 1941 (Isley Brothers)

Leo Sayer / 1948 ("When I Need You")

Stan Lynch / 1955 (Tom Petty & the Heartbreakers)

Mike Barson / 1958 (Madness)

May 22

Bernie Taupin / 1950 (songwriter with Elton John: "Daniel")

Iva Davies / 1955 (Icehouse)

Patrick Morrissey / 1959 (The Smiths)

May 23

"The Kids Are Alright" / 1979 (New York debut of film by The Who)

May 24

Bob Dylan / 1941 ("Lay Lady Lay")

Patti LaBelle / 1944 (Patti LaBelle & the Bluebelles/LaBelle)

Derek Quinn / 1942 (Freddie & the Dreamers)

May 25

Mitch Margo / 1947 (The Tokens)

Paul Weller / 1958 (The Jam/The Style Council)

Miles Davis / 1925 (legendary jazz trumpeter)

May 26

Stevie Nicks / 1948 (Fleetwood Mac)

Levon Helm / 1942 (The Band)

May 27

Cilla Black / 1943 ("It's for You")

Siouxsie Siouxsie / 1957 (Siouxsie & the Banshees)

Neil Finn / 1958 (Split Enz)

MAY 28

Gladys Knight / 1944 (Gladys Knight & the Pips)

John Fogerty / 1945 (Creedence Clearwater Revival)

Kylie Minogue / 1968 ("The Locomotion")

MAY 29

Melissa Etheridge / 1961 ("I'm the Only One")

Rebbie Jackson / 1950 ("Centipede")

Gary Brooker / 1945 (Procol Harum)

Mel Gaynor / 1959 (Simple Minds)

MAY 30

Lenny Davidson / 1944 (The Dave Clark Five)

Nicky Headon / 1955 (The Clash)

MAY 31

Peter Yarrow / 1938 (Peter, Paul & Mary)

John Bonham / 1948 (Led Zeppelin)

Mick Ralphs / 1944 (Mott the Hoople)

JUNE 1

Pat Boone / 1934 ("Love Letters in the Sand")

Graham Russell / 1950 (Air Supply)

Ron Wood / 1947 (The Jeff Beck Group/Faces/The Rolling Stones)

Mike Joyce / 1963 (The Smiths)

JUNE 2

William Guest / 1941 (Gladys Knight & the Pips)

Charlie Watts / 1941 (The Rolling Stones)

Bob Benrit / 1945 (Argent)

Tony Hadley / 1959 (Spandau Ballet)

JUNE 3

Curtis Mayfield / 1942 ("Freddie's Dead")

Michael Clarke / 1943 (The Byrds)

Suzi Quatro / 1950 ("Stumblin' In")

Deniece Williams / 1951 ("Let's Hear It for the Boy')

John Paul Jones / 1946 (Led Zeppelin)

JUNE 4

Michelle Phillips / 1945 (The Mamas & the Papas)

El DeBarge / 1961 ("Who's Johnny")

Gordon Waller / 1945 (Peter & Gordon)

Roger Ball / 1944 (Average White Band)

JUNE 5

Laurie Anderson / 1947 ("O Superman")

Michael McBain / 1954 (Iron Maiden)

JUNE 6

Levi Stubbs / 1936 (The Four Tops)

Gary U.S. Bonds / 1939 ("New Orleans")

JUNE 7

Prince / 1958 ("Purple Rain")

Tom Jones / 1940 ("It's Not Unusual")

JUNE 8

Nancy Sinatra / 1940 ("These Boots Are Made for Walkin' ")

Boz Scaggs / 1944 ("Low Down")

Neil Mitchell / 1967 (Wet Wet Wet)

Rob Pilatus / 1964 (Milli Vanilli)

The Four Tops: *(Left to right)* Lawrence Payton; Abdul Fakir—December 26; Levi Stubbs—June 6; Obie Benson

JUNE 9

Jackie Wilson / 1934 ("Reet Petite")

Jon Lord / 1941 (Deep Purple)

Les Paul / 1915 ("How High the Moon")

JUNE 10

Shirley Owens Alston / 1941 (The Shirelles)

Rick Price / 1944 (The Move)

JUNE 11

Joey Dee / 1940 (Joey Dee & the Starlighters)

Skip Allen / 1948 (The Pretty Things)

JUNE 12

Len Barry / 1942 (The Dovells)

Brad Delp / 1951 (Boston)

Reg Presley / 1943 (The Troggs)

Bun E. Carlos / 1953 (Cheap Trick)

JUNE 13

Bobby Freeman / 1940 ("Do You Wanna Dance?")

Danny Klein / 1946 (The J. Geils Band)

Deniecee Pearson / 1968 (Five Star)

Dennis Locorriere / 1949 (Dr. Hook & the Medicine Show)

JUNE 14

Boy George / 1961 (Culture Club)

Rod Argent / 1945 (The Zombies)

Culture Club: *(Left to right)* John Moss—September 11; Boy George—June 14; Mikey Craig—February 15, Roy Hay—August 12

Jimmy Lea / 1952 (Slade)

Muff Winwood / 1943 (The Spencer Davis Group)

JUNE 15

Harry Nilsson / 1941 ("Without You")

Russell Hitchcock / 1949 (Air Supply)

Brad Gillis / 1957 (Night Ranger)

Waylon Jennings / 1937 (bass player for Buddy Holly & the Crickets)

JUNE 16

Paula Abdul / 1962 ("Forever Your Girl")

Lamont Dozier / 1941 (one third of Motown producing/writing team
Holland/Dozier/Holland)

JUNE 17

Barry Manilow / 1946 ("Mandy")

JUNE 18

Paul McCartney / 1942 (The Beatles)

Alison Moyet / 1961 ("Love Resurrection")

Tom Bailey / 1957 (The Thompson Twins)

JUNE 19

Ann Wilson / 1951 (Heart)

Tommy DeVito / 1936 (The Four Seasons)

Spanky McFarlane / 1942 (Spanky & Our Gang)

JUNE 20

Cyndi Lauper / 1953 ("True Colors")

Brian Wilson / 1942 (The Beach Boys)

Lionel Richie / 1949 ("Hello")

Michael Anthony / 1955 (Van Halen)

Eilly Guy / 1936 (The Coasters)

JUNE 21

Ray Davies / 1944 (The Kinks)

Joey Kramer / 1950 (Aerosmith)

Nils Lofgren / 1951 ("Cry Tough")

Joey Molland / 1948 (Badfinger)

JUNE 22

Todd Rundgren / 1948 ("Hello, It's Me")

Peter Asher / 1944 (Peter & Gordon)

Tom Cunningham / 1965 (Wet Wet Wet)

Howard Kaylan / 1945 (The Turtles)

JUNE 23

Richard Coles / 1962 (The Communards)

Paul Goddard / 1945 (The Atlanta Rhythm Section)

JUNE 24

Eddie Floyd / 1935 ("Knock on Wood")

JUNE 26

Billy Davis Jr. / 1940 (The Fifth Dimension)

Mick Jones / 1955 (The Clash)

Georgie Fame / 1943 ("The Ballad of Bonnie and Clyde")

JUNE 27

Bruce Johnston / 1944 (The Beach Boys)

JUNE 28

Bobby Harrison / 1943 (Procol Harum)

Dave Knights / 1945 (Procol Harum)

JUNE 29

Little Eva / 1945 ("The Locomotion")

Ian Paice / 1948 (Deep Purple)

Johnny Ace / 1929 ("Pledging My Love")

Stedman Pearson / 1964 (Five Star)

JUNE 30

Florence Ballard / 1943 (The Supremes)

Hal Lindes / 1952 (Dire Straits)

Andy Scott / 1951 (Sweet)

Glenn Shorrock / 1944 (The Little River Band)

JULY 1

Fred Schneider / 1951 (The B-52's)

Debbie Harry / 1945 (Blondie)

Delaney Bramlett / 1939 (Delaney & Bonnie)

Bobby Day / 1934 ("Rockin' Robin")

JULY 2

Paul Williams / 1939 (The Temptations)

Johnny Colla / 1952 (Huey Lewis & the News)

JULY 3

Fontella Bass / 1940 ("Rescue Me")

Laura Branigan / 1957 ("Gloria")

Steve Pearcy / 1959 (Ratt)

Mike Corby / 1955 (The Babys)

Fred Schneider of The B-52's—July 1; and Mary Wilson—March 6, at the 1995 Pioneer Awards of The Rhythm & Blues Foundation

JULY 4

Bill Withers / 1938 ("Lean on Me")

Jeremy Spencer / 1948 (Fleetwood Mac)

Al Wilson / 1943 (Canned Heat)

John Waite / 1954 (The Babys)

JULY 5

Huey Lewis / 1950 (Huey Lewis & the News)

Robbie Robertson / 1944 (The Band)

Michael Monarch / 1950 (Steppenwolf)

JULY 6

Bill Haley / 1925 (Bill Haley & His Comets)

Gene Chandler / 1937 ("The Duke of Earl")

Jesse Harms / 1952 (REO Speedwagon)

John Keeble / 1959 (Spandau Ballet)

JULY 7

Ringo Starr / 1940 (The Beatles)

Warren Entner / 1944 (The Grass Roots)

Jim Rodford / 1945 (Argent)

JULY 8

Graham Jones / 1961 (Haircut 100)

Jaimoe Johnny Johnson / 1944 (The Allman Brothers Band)

JULY 9

Debbie Sledge / 1954 (Sister Sledge)

Marc Almond / 1959 (Soft Cell)

Bon Scott / 1946 (AC/DC)

Jim Kerr / 1959 (Simple Minds)

JULY 10

Arlo Guthrie / 1947 ("Alice's Restaurant")
Neil Tennant / 1954 (The Pet Shop Boys)
Jerry Miller / 1943 (Moby Grape)

JULY 11

Ruth Pointer / 1951 (The Pointer Sisters)
Richie Sambora / 1959 (Bon Jovi)
Terry Garthwaite / 1938 (The Joy of Cooking)

JULY 12

Christine McVie / 1943 (Fleetwood Mac)
John Wetton / 1949 (Asia)

JULY 13

Roger McGuinn / 1942 (The Byrds)
Stephen Jo Bladd / 1942 (The J. Geils Band)
Mark Mendoza / 1956 (Twisted Sister)

JULY 14

Chris Cross / 1952 (Ultravox)
Woody Guthrie / 1912 (folk pioneer: "This Land Is Your Land")

JULY 15

Linda Ronstadt / 1946 ("You're No Good")
Millie Jackson / 1943 ("Hurts So Good")
Peter Lewis / 1945 (Moby Grape)

JULY 16

Stewart Copeland / 1952 (The Police)

Tony Jackson / 1940 (The Searchers)

JULY 17

Phoebe Snow / 1952 ("Poetry Man")

Spencer Davis / 1942 (The Spencer Davis Group)

Chet McCracken / 1952 (The Doobie Brothers)

Bill Ward / 1949 (Black Sabbath)

JULY 18

Martha Reeves / 1941 (Martha & the Vandellas)

Dion DiMucci / 1939 (Dion & the Belmonts)

"Papa Dee" Allen / 1931 (War)

Screamin' Jan Hawkins / 1929 ("I Put a Spell on You")

JULY 19

Bernie Leadon / 1947 (The Eagles)

Brian May / 1947 (Queen)

Alan Gorrie / 1946 (The Average White Band)

JULY 20

Kim Carnes / 1946 ("Bette Davis Eyes")

John Lodge / 1945 (The Moody Blues)

Carlos Santana / 1947 (Santana)

Jay Jay French / 1954 (Twisted Sister)

JULY 21

Cat Stevens / 1948 ("Peace Train")

Barry Whitham / 1946 (Herman's Hermits)

JULY 22

Estelle Bennett / 1944 (The Ronettes)

Don Henley / 1947 (The Eagles)

Richard Davies / 1944 (Supertramp)

George Clinton / 1940 (The Parliaments)

JULY 23

David Essex / 1947 ("Rock On")

Dino Dinelli / 1945 (The Rascals)

Martin Gore / 1961 (Depeche Mode)

Andy Mackay / 1946 (Roxy Music)

JULY 24

Mick Fleetwood / 1947 (Fleetwood Mac)

Jim Armstrong / 1944 (Them)

Mick Karn / 1958 (Japan)

Robbie Grey / 1957 (Modern English)

JULY 25

Jim McCarty / 1943 (The Yardbirds)

Verdine White / 1951 (Earth, Wind & Fire)

JULY 26

Mick Jagger / 1943 (The Rolling Stones)

Roger Taylor / 1949 (Queen)

JULY 27

Bobbie Gentry / 1944 ("Ode to Billy Joe")

Al Ramsey / 1943 (Gary Lewis & the Playboys)

JULY 28

Rick Wright / 1945 (Pink Floyd)

Simon Kirke / 1949 (Bad Company)

Andy Fraser / 1948 (Free)

Mike Bloomfield / 1944 (blues guitarist)

JULY 29

Geddy Lee / 1953 (Rush)

Neal Doughty / 1946 (REO Speedwagon)

Charlie Christian / 1916 (electric guitar pioneer)

JULY 30

Kate Bush / 1958 ("Wuthering Heights")

Paul Anka / 1941 ("Puppy Love")

JULY 31

Bob Welch / 1946 (Fleetwood Mac)

Gary Lewis / 1946 (Gary Lewis & the Playboys)

John West / 1939 (Gary Lewis & the Playboys)

AUGUST 1

Jerry Garcia / 1942 (The Grateful Dead)

Joe Elliot / 1959 (Def Leppard)

Ricky Coonce / 1947 (The Grass Roots)

AUGUST 2

Garth Hudson / 1943 (The Band)

Doris Coley / 1941 (The Shirelles)

Edward Patten / 1939 (Gladys Knight & the Pips)

Andrew Gold / 1951 ("Thank You for Being a Friend")

Pete De Freitas / 1961 (Echo & the Bunnymen)

AUGUST 3

Beverly Lee / 1941 (The Shirelles)

B.B. Dickerson / 1949 (War)

AUGUST 4

Frankie Ford / 1940 ("Sea Cruise")

Paul Layton / 1947 (The New Seekers)

AUGUST 5

Pete Burns / 1959 (Dead or Alive)

Eddie Ojeda / 1954 (Twisted Sister)

Rick Huxley / 1942 (The Dave Clark Five)

AUGUST 6

Isaac Hayes / 1938 ("Shaft")

Mike Elliot / 1939 (The Foundations)

AUGUST 7

Bruce Dickinson / 1958 (Iron Maiden)

Jacqui O'Sullivan / 1960 (Bananarama)

AUGUST 8

The Edge / 1961 (U2)

Denis Payton / 1943 (The Dave Clark Five)

Paul Jackson / 1961 (T' Pau)

Chris Foreman / 1958 (Madness)

AUGUST 9

Whitney Houston / 1963 ("I Will Always Love You")

Kurtis Blow / 1959 ("If I Ruled the World")

Viv Prince / 1944 (The Pretty Things)

AUGUST 10

Ronnie Spector / 1943 (The Ronettes)

Ron Hay / 1961 (Culture Club)

AUGUST 13

Dan Fogelberg / 1951 ("Same Auld Lang Syne")

Tony Santini / 1948 (Sha Na Na)

AUGUST 14

David Crosby / 1941 (The Byrds/Crosby, Stills & Nash)

Dash Crofts / 1940 (Seals & Crofts)

Larry Graham / 1946 (Sly & the Family Stone)

August 15

Pete York / 1942 (The Spencer Davis Group)

Adam Yauch / 1967 (The Beastie Boys)

Jimmy Webb / 1946 (songwriter: "MacArthur Park")

Billy Pinkney / 1925 (The Drifters)

August 16

Madonna / 1959 ("Like a Prayer")

Gordon Fleet / 1945 (The Easybeats)

August 17

Belinda Carlisle / 1958 (The Go-Go's)

Kevin Rowland / 1953 (Dexy's Midnight Runners)

Gary Talley / 1947 (Big Star)

Sib Hashian / 1949 (Boston)

August 18

Nona Hendryx / 1945 (Patti LaBelle & the Bluebelles/Labelle)

Dennis Elliot / 1950 (Foreigner)

Carl Wayne / 1944 (The Move/Electric Light Orchestra)

Nigel Griggs / 1949 (Split Enz)

August 19

Johnny Nash / 1940 ("I Can See Clearly Now")

Tan Gillan / 1945 (Deep Purple)

Ginger Baker / 1940 (Cream)

Donnie Wahlberg / 1970 (New Kids on the Block)

August 20

Robert Plant / 1948 (Led Zeppelin)

Phil Lynott / 1951 (Thin Lizzy)

Doug Fieger / 1957 (The Knack)

August 21

Jackie DeShannon / 1944 ("What the World Needs Now Is Love")

Kenny Rogers / 1938 (The First Edition)

Steve Smith / 1954 (Journey)

Kim Sledge / 1957 (Sister Sledge)

August 22

Roland Orzabel / 1961 (Tears for Fears)

John Lee Hooker / 1917 (blues pioneer)

Debbie Peterson / 1961 (The Bangles)

August 23

Keith Moon / 1947 (The Who)

Rick Springfield / 1949 ("Jessie's Girl")

August 24

Jim Capladi / 1944 (Traffic)

Joe Chambers / 1942 (The Chambers Brothers)

Mark Bedford / 1961 (Madness)

Malcolm Duncan / 1945 (The Average White Band)

AUGUST 25

Gene Simmons / 1950 (KISS)

Elvis Costello / 1955 ("My Aim Is True")

Rob Halford / 1951 (Judas Priest)

AUGUST 26

Valerie Simpson / 1948 (Ashford & Simpson)

Fred Milano / 1940 (Dion & the Belmonts)

Michael Chetwood / 1954 (T' Pau)

Chris Curtis / 1941 (The Searchers)

Ashford & Simpson: Valerie Simpson—August 26; Nicholas Ashford—May 4

August 27

Daryl Dragon / 1942 (The Captain & Tennille)

Tim Bogert / 1944 (Vanilla Fudge)

Alex Lifeson / 1953 (Rush)

August 28

Wayne Osmond / 1951 (The Osmonds)

Ann Lantree / 1943 (The Honeycombs)

August 29

Michael Jackson / 1958 ("Beat It")

Chris Copping / 1945 (Procol Harum)

August 30

John Phillips / 1935 (The Mamas & the Papas)

John McNally / 1941 (The Searchers)

August 31

Van Morrison / 1945 ("Moondance")

Debbie Gibson / 1970 ("Foolish Beat")

Glenn Tilbrook / 1957 (Squeeze)

Tony DeFranco / 1959 (The DeFranco Family)

September 1

Gloria Estefan / 1957 (Miami Sound Machine)

Barry Gibb / 1946 (The Bee Gees)

Bruce Foxton / 1955 (The Jam)

SEPTEMBER 2

Rosalind Ashford / 1943 (Martha & the Vandellas)

Steve Procaro / 1957 (Toto)

Sam Gordon / 1939 (The Impressions)

SEPTEMBER 3

Al Jardine / 1942 (The Beach Boys)

Donald Brewer / 1948 (Grand Funk Railroad)

Eric Bell / 1947 (Thin Lizzy)

Steve Jones / 1955 (The Sex Pistols)

SEPTEMBER 4

Merald "Bubba" Knight / 1942 (Gladys Knight & the Pips)

Gary Duncan / 1946 (Quicksilver Messenger Service)

Greg Elmore / 1946 (Quicksilver Messenger Service)

SEPTEMBER 5

Freddie Mercury / 1946 (Queen)

Al Stewart / 1945 ("The Year of the Cat")

Dean Ford / 1946 (Marmalade)

Buddy Miles / 1946 (Jimi Hendrix's drummer/The Buddy Miles Band)

SEPTEMBER 6

Roger Waters / 1944 (Pink Floyd)

Claydes Smith / 1948 (Kool & the Gang)

Pal Waaktar / 1961 (A-Ha)

Jimmy Reed / 1925 ("Honest I Do")

SEPTEMBER 7

Buddy Holly / 1936 (Buddy Holly & the Crickets)

Chrissie Hynde / 1951 (The Pretenders)

Benmont Tench / 1952 (Tom Petty & the Heartbreakers)

SEPTEMBER 8

Ron McKernan (Pigpen)/ 1945 (The Grateful Dead)

David Lewis / 1958 (Atlantic Starr)

Sal Valentino / 1942 (The Beau Brummels)

Dean Daughtry / 1946 (Atlanta Rhythm Section)

Jimmy Rodgers / 1897 (rock-a-billy pioneer)

SEPTEMBER 9

Billy Preston / 1946 ("Will It Go Round in Circles")

Otis Redding / 1941 ("Sitting on the Dock of the Bay")

Dave Stewart / 1952 (Eurythmics)

Roger Waters / 1944 (Pink Floyd)

Lol Creme / 1947 (10cc/Godfrey & Creme)

SEPTEMBER 10

Jose Feliciano / 1945 ("Light My Fire")

Joe Perry / 1950 (Journey)

Siobahan Fahey / 1957 (Bananarama)

Don Powell / 1950 (Slade)

SEPTEMBER 11

Jermaine Jackson / 1954 (The Jackson Five)

Jon Moss / 1957 (Culture Club)

Bernie Dwyer / 1940 (Freddie & the Dreamers)

Mick Talbot / 1958 (The Style Council)

SEPTEMBER 12

Maria Muldaur / 1943 ("Midnight at the Oasis")

Gerry Beckley / 1952 (America)

Barry White / 1944 ("Can't Get Enough of Your Love, Babe")

Brian Robertson / 1956 (Thin Lizzy)

Neil Pearl / 1952 (Rush)

SEPTEMBER 13

Randy Jones / 1952 (Village People)

David Clayton-Thomas / 1941 (Blood, Sweat & Tears)

Peter Cetera / 1944 (Chicago)

Ray Elliot / 1943 (Them)

SEPTEMBER 14

Paul Kossoff / 1950 (Free)

Morten Harket / 1959 (A-Ha)

SEPTEMBER 15

Lee Dorman / 1945 (Iron Butterfly)

SEPTEMBER 16

Betty Kelly / 1944 (Martha & the Vandellas)

B.B. King / 1925 ("The Thrill Is Gone")

Kenny Jones / 1948 (Faces/The Who)

Joe Butler / 1943 (The Lovin' Spoonful)

Ron Blair / 1952 (Tom Petty & the Heartbreakers)

SEPTEMBER 17

Lamonte McLemore / 1939 (The Fifth Dimension)

Hank Williams / 1923 ("Your Cheatin' Heart")

"Fee" Waybill / 1950 (The Tubes)

SEPTEMBER 18

Frankie Avalon / 1940 ("Venus")

Dee Dee Ramone / 1952 (The Ramones)

Kerry Livgren / 1949 (Kansas)

SEPTEMBER 19

Cass Elliot / 1941 (The Mamas & the Papas)

Brian Epstein / 1934 (manager of The Beatles)

Nile Rogers / 1952 (Chic)

Bill Medley / 1940 (The Righteous Brothers)

SEPTEMBER 20

Alannah Currie / 1959 (The Thompson Twins)

John Panozzo / 1947 (Styx)

Chuck Panozzo / 1947 (Styx)

SEPTEMBER 21

Phil Taylor / 1954 (Motorhead)

Leonard Cohen / 1934 (songwriter: "Suzanne")

Joan Jett—September 22

SEPTEMBER 22

Joan Jett / 1960 (The Runaways/Joan Jett & the Blackhearts)

Debby Boone / 1956 ("You Light Up My Life")

David Coverdale / 1949 (Whitesnake)

SEPTEMBER 23

Bruce Springsteen / 1949 ("The Streets of Philadelphia")

Ray Charles / 1930 ("I Can't Stop Loving You")

Ronald Bushy / 1945 (Iron Butterfly)

Steve Boone / 1943 (The Lovin' Spoonful)

Neal Smith / 1947 (Alice Cooper)

September 24

Linda McCartney / 1942 (Wings)

Gerry Marsden / 1942 (Gerry & the Pacemakers)

Barbara Allbut / 1940 (The Angels)

September 25

Joseph Jesse Russell / 1939 (The Persuasions)

John Locke / 1943 (Spirit)

Onnie McIntyre / 1945 (Average White Band)

September 26

Olivia Newton-John / 1948 ("Physical")

Brian Ferry / 1945 (Roxy Music)

Craig Chaquico / 1954 (Jefferson Starship)

September 27

Meat Loaf / 1948 ("Paradise by the Dashboard Light")

Shaun Cassidy / 1959 ("That's Rock 'n' Roll")

Randy Bachman / 1943 (Bachman-Turner Overdrive)

September 28

Ben E. King / 1938 ("Stand By Me")

Nick St. Nicholas / 1943 (Steppenwolf)

September 29

Jerry Lee Lewis / 1935 ("Great Balls o' Fire")

Mark Farner / 1948 (Grand Funk Railroad)

September 30

Marilyn McCoo / 1943 (The Fifth Dimension)

Frankie Lyman / 1942 (Frankie Lyman & the Teenagers)

Johnny Mathis / 1935 ("Wonderful Wonderful")

Marc Bolan / 1947 (T. Rex)

October 1

Donny Hathaway / 1945 ("Where Is the Love" with Roberta Flack)

Howard Hewett / 1957 (Shalamar)

October 2

Sting / 1951 (The Police)

Don McLean / 1945 ("American Pie")

Tiffany / 1971 ("I Think We're Alone Now")

Philip Oakey / 1955 (The Human League)

October 3

Chubby Checker / 1941 ("Let's Twist Again")

Lindsey Buckingham / 1949 (Fleetwood Mac)

Stevie Ray Vaughan / 1954 ("Voodoo Chile")

Eddie Cochran / 1938 ("Summertime Blues")

October 4

Helen Reddy / 1942 ("Delta Dawn")

Chris Lowe / 1959 (The Pet Shop Boys)

OCTOBER 5

Steve Miller / 1943 ("Abracadabra")

Bob Geldof / 1954 (The Boomtown Rats)

Richard Street / 1942 (The Temptations)

Carlo Mastrangelo / 1939 (Dion & the Belmonts)

OCTOBER 6

Kevin Cronin / 1951 (REO Speedwagon)

Tim Burgess / 1961 (T' Pau)

OCTOBER 7

John Cougar Mellencamp / 1951 ("Pink Houses")

Tico Torres / 1953 (Bon Jovi)

Kevin Godley / 1945 (10cc/Godley & Creme)

Martin Murray / 1941 (The Honeycombs)

OCTOBER 8

Johnny Ramone / 1948 (The Ramones)

Hamish Stuart / 1949 (Average White Band)

Tony Wilson / 1947 (Hot Chocolate)

Robert "Kool" Bell / 1950 (Kool & the Gang)

OCTOBER 9

John Lennon / 1940 (The Beatles)

John Entwisle / 1944 (The Who)

Jackson Browne / 1948 ("Doctor My Eyes")

Peter Tosh / 1944 ("[You Got to Walk and] Don't Look Back")

OCTOBER 10

David Lee Roth / 1955 (Van Halen)

Midge Ure / 1953 (Ultravox)

Martin Kemp / 1961 (Spandau Ballet)

Denis D'Ell / 1943 (The Honeycombs)

OCTOBER 11

Daryl Hall / 1949 (Hall & Oates)

Gary Mallaber / 1946 (The Steve Miller Band)

Greg Douglas / 1949 (The Steve Miller Band)

Blair Cunningham / 1957 (Haircut 100)

OCTOBER 12

Melvin Franklin / 1942 (The Temptations)

Sam Moore / 1935 (Sam & Dave)

Rick Parfitt / 1948 (Status Quo)

OCTOBER 13

Paul Simon / 1942 ("50 Ways to Leave Your Lover")

Sammy Hagar / 1947 (Van Halen)

Chris Farlowe / 1940 (The Thunderbirds)

OCTOBER 14

Cliff Richard / 1940 ("Devil Woman")

Justin Hayward / 1946 (The Moody Blues)

Thomas Dolby / 1958 ("She Blinded Me with Science")

A. J. Pero / 1959 (Twisted Sister)

OCTOBER 15

Richard Carpenter / 1946 (The Carpenters)

Don Stevenson / 1942 (Moby Grape)

Chris De Burgh / 1950 ("Lady in Red")

Tito Jackson / 1953 (The Jackson Five)

OCTOBER 16

Bob Weir / 1947 (The Grateful Dead)

Fred Turner / 1943 (Bachman-Turner Overdrive)

Gary Kemp / 1960 (Spandau Ballet)

OCTOBER 17

Jim Seals / 1941 (Seals & Crofts)

Jim Tucker / 1946 (The Turtles)

Alan Howard / 1941 (The Tremeloes)

Gary Puckett / 1942 (Gary Puckett & the Union Gap)

OCTOBER 18

Chuck Berry / 1926 ("Maybellene")

Keith Knudsen / 1952 (The Doobie Brothers)

Gary Richrath / 1949 (REO Speedwagon)

OCTOBER 19

Peter Max / 1937 (graphic and album cover artist par excellence)

Jennifer Holliday / 1960 ("And I Am Telling You I'm Not Going")

October 20

Tom Petty / 1953 (Tom Petty & the Heartbreakers)

Ric Lee / 1945 (Ten Years After)

Jay Siegel / 1939 (The Tokens)

October 21

Manfred Mann / 1940 ("The Mighty Quinn")

Steve Cropper / 1941 (Booker T. & the M.G.'s)

Steve Lukather / 1957 (Toto)

October 22

Annette Funicello / 1942 ("Tall Paul")

Leslie West / 1945 (Mountain)

Bobby Fuller / 1942 (The Bobby Fuller Four)

Eddie Brigati / 1946 (The Rascals)

Ray Jones / 1939 (Billy J. Kramer & the Dakotas)

October 23

Ellie Greenwich / 1940 (songwriter: "Leader of the Pack")

"Weird" Al Yankovic / 1959 ("Eat It")

Greg Ridley / 1947 (Humble Pie)

Freddie Marsden / 1940 (Gerry & the Pacemakers)

October 24

Bill Wyman / 1936 (The Rolling Stones)

Jerry Edmonton / 1946 (Steppenwolf)

Dale "Buffin" Griffin / 1948 (Mott the Hoople)

(Second from left) Jon Anderson of Yes—October 25; with Rick Wakeman *(left)*—May 18; Bill Bruford *(right)*—May 17; Steve Howe *(far right)*—April 8

OCTOBER 25

Jon Anderson / 1944 (Yes)

Jon Hall / 1947 (Orleans)

OCTOBER 26

Keith Strickland / 1953 (The B-52's)

Keith Hopwood / 1946 (Herman's Hermits)

October 27

Simon Le Bon / 1958 (Duran Duran)

Byron Allred / 1948 (The Steve Miller Band)

October 28

Wayne Fontana / 1940 (Wayne Fontana & the Mindbenders)

Stephen Morris / 1957 (New Order)

October 29

Big Bopper / 1932 ("Chantilly Lace")

Denny Laine / 1944 (The Moody Blues/Wings)

Peter Green / 1946 (Fleetwood Mac)

Kevin DuBrow / 1955 (Quiet Riot)

October 30

Grace Slick / 1939 (Jefferson Airplane/Starship)

Otis Williams / 1949 (The Temptations)

Timothy B. Schmit / 1947 (Poco/The Eagles)

Eddie Holland / 1939 (one third of Motown producing/writing trio
Holland/Dozier/Holland)

October 31

Bernard Edwards / 1952 (Chic)

Russ Ballard / 1947 (Argent)

Adam Horovitz / 1966 (The Beastie Boys)

Larry Mullen Jr. / 1961 (U2)

NOVEMBER 1

Rick Grech / 1946 (Traffic)

Ronald Bell / 1951 (Kool & the Gang)

Rick Allen / 1963 (Def Leppard)

Mags Furuholmen / 1962 (A-Ha)

NOVEMBER 2

Jay Black / 1941 (Jay & the Americans)

Keith Emerson / 1944 (Emerson, Lake & Palmer)

Dave Pegg / 1947 (Fairport Convention)

Earl Carroll / 1937 (The Cadillacs)

NOVEMBER 3

Lulu / 1948 ("To Sir with Love")

Adam Ant / 1954 (Adam & the Ants)

Brian Poole / 1941 (The Tremeloes)

NOVEMBER 4

Chris Difford / 1954 (Squeeze)

Delbert McClinton / 1940 ("Giving It Up for Your Love")

NOVEMBER 5

Bryan Adams / 1959 ("Cuts Like a Knife")

Ike Turner / 1931 (Ike & Tina Turner)

Peter Noone / 1947 (Herman's Hermits)

Art Garfunkel / 1941 (Simon & Garfunkel)

NOVEMBER 6

Glenn Frey / 1948 (The Eagles)

P. J. Proby / 1938 ("Hold Me")

George Young / 1947 (The Easybeats)

Doug Sahm / 1941 (Sir Douglas Quintet)

NOVEMBER 7

Joni Mitchell / 1943 ("Help Me")

Mary Travers / 1937 (Peter, Paul & Mary)

Johnny Rivers / 1942 ("Poor Side of Town")

NOVEMBER 8

Bonnie Raitt / 1949 ("You Got It")

Ricki Lee Jones / 1954 ("Chuck E's in Love")

Bonnie Bramlett / 1944 (Delaney & Bonnie)

Roy Wood / 1946 (The Electric Light Orchestra)

Bonnie Raitt—November 8, with Martha Reeves—July 18, brought together for the 1995 Rhythm & Blues Foundation's Pioneer Awards

November 9

Tom Fogerty / 1941 (Creedence Clearwater Revival)

Dennis Stratton / 1954 (Iron Maiden)

Alan Gratzer / 1948 (REO Speedwagon)

Phil May / 1944 (The Pretty Things)

November 10

Greg Lake / 1948 (Emerson, Lake & Palmer)

Mario Cipollina / 1954 (Huey Lewis & the News)

November 11

LaVern Baker / 1929 ("Tweedlee Dee")

Chris Dreja / 1945 (The Yardbirds)

Vince Martell / 1945 (Vanilla Fudge)

Ian Craig Marsh / 1956 (Heaven 17/ The Human League)

Chip Hawkes / 1946 (The Tremeloes)

Jesse Colin Young / 1944 (The Youngbloods)

November 12

Neil Young / 1945 ("Heart of Gold")

Brian Hyland / 1943 ("Gypsy Woman")

Leslie McKeown / 1955 (The Bay City Rollers)

Errol Brown / 1948 (Hot Chocolate)

Jimmy Hayes / 1943 (The Persuasions)

November 13

Bill Gibson / 1951 (Huey Lewis & the News)

Baby Washington / 1940 ("That's How Heartaches Are Made")

NOVEMBER 14

Freddie Garrity / 1940 (Freddie & the Dreamers)

James Young / 1948 (Styx)

Alec John Such / 1952 (Bon Jovi)

NOVEMBER 15

Petula Clark / 1932 ("Don't Sleep in the Subway")

Clyde McPhatter/ 1933 (The Drifters)

Frida Lygstad / 1945 (ABBA)

NOVEMBER 16

Toni Brown / 1938 (The Joy of Cooking)

Patti Santos / 1949 (It's a Beautiful Day)

NOVEMBER 17

Gordon Lightfoot / 1938 ("If You Could Read My Mind")

Gene Clark / 1944 (The Byrds)

Bob Gaudio / 1942 (The Four Seasons)

Martin Barre / 1946 (Jethro Tull)

NOVEMBER 18

Hank Ballard / 1936 ("Kansas City")

Graham Parker / 1950 (Graham Parker & the Rumor)

John McFee / 1953 (Clover/The Doobie Brothers)

Kim Wilde / 1960 ("Say You Really Want Me")

NOVEMBER 19

Pete Moore / 1939 (The Miracles)

Fred Lipsius / 1943 (Blood, Sweat & Tears)

Hank Medress / 1938 (The Tokens)

NOVEMBER 20

Norman Greenbaum / 1942 ("Spirit in the Sky")

Duane Allman / 1946 (The Allman Brothers Band)

Joe Walsh / 1947 (The James Gang /The Eagles)

George Grantham / 1947 (Poco)

Michael Diamond / 1965 (The Beastie Boys)

NOVEMBER 21

Dr. John / 1941 ("Right Place but the Wrong Time")

Lonnie Jordan / 1948 (War)

Livingston Taylor / 1950 ("First Time Love")

NOVEMBER 22

Floyd Sneed / 1943 (Three Dog Night)

Tina Weymouth / 1950 (Talking Heads)

Aston Barrett / 1946 (Bob Marley & the Wailers)

Delphine Reeves / 1951 (Martha Reeves & the Vandellas)

NOVEMBER 23

Bruce Hornsby / 1954 (Bruce Hornsby & the Range)

Freddie Marsden / 1940 (Gerry & the Pacemakers)

NOVEMBER 24

Lee Michaels / 1945 ("Do You Know What I Mean")

Donald "Duck" Dunn / 1941 (Booker T. & the MG's)

Chris Hayes / 1957 (Huey Lewis & the News)

Bev Bevan / 1946 (Electric Light Orchestra)

NOVEMBER 25

Percy Sledge / 1940 ("When a Man Loves a Woman")

Amy Grant / 1960 ("Baby Baby")

Steve Rothery / 1959 (Marillion)

NOVEMBER 26

Tina Turner / 1939 ("What's Love Got to Do with It")

Jean Terrell / 1944 (replaced Diana Ross in The Supremes)

John McVie / 1945 (Fleetwood Mac)

Alan Henderson / 1944 (Them)

NOVEMBER 27

Jimi Hendrix / 1942 ("Purple Haze")

Al Jackson / 1935 (Booker T. & the MG's)

Charlie Burchill / 1959 (Simple Minds)

NOVEMBER 28

Berry Gordy Jr. / 1929 (president and founder of Motown Records)

Randy Newman / 1943 (songwriter: "Mama Told Me Not to Come")

Beeb Birtles / 1948 (The Little River Band)

NOVEMBER 29

Denny Doherty / 1941 (The Mamas & the Papas)

Felix Cavaliere / 1944 (The Rascals)

John Mayall / 1943 ("Don't Waste My Time")

Barry Goudreau / 1951 (Boston)

NOVEMBER 30

Dick Clark / 1929 (host: "American Bandstand")

Paul Stookey / 1937 (Peter, Paul & Mary)

Billy Idol / 1955 ("White Wedding")

George McArdle / 1954 (The Little River Band)

Leo Lyons / 1944 (Ten Years After)

DECEMBER 1

Bette Midler / 1945 ("The Rose")

John Densmore / 1945 (The Doors)

Gilbert O'Sullivan / 1946 ("Alone Again, Naturally")

Lou Rawls / 1935 ("You'll Never Find Another Love Like Mine")

Billy Paul / 1934 ("Me and Mrs. Jones")

DECEMBER 2

Tom McGuiness / 1941 (Manfred Mann)

Rick Savage / 1960 (Def Leppard)

DECEMBER 3

Ozzy Osbourne / 1948 (Black Sabbath)

John Cale / 1940 (The Velvet Underground")

DECEMBER 4

Dennis Wilson / 1944 (The Beach Boys)

Chris Hillman / 1942 (The Byrds)

Bob Mosley / 1942 (Moby Grape)

Freddy Cannon / 1940 ("Palisades Park")

Bette Midler—December 1

DECEMBER 5

Jim Messina / 1947 (Poco/Loggins & Messina)

J.J. Cale / 1938 ("Crazy Mama")

Les Nemes / 1960 (Haircut 100)

DECEMBER 6

Mike Smith / 1943 (The Dave Clark Five)

Rick Buckler / 1955 (The Jam)

DECEMBER 7

Harry Chapin / 1942 ("Taxi")

Tom Waits / 1949 ("Looking for the Heart of Saturday Night")

DECEMBER 8

Gregg Allman / 1947 (The Allman Brothers Band)

Jim Morrison / 1943 (The Doors)

Paul Rutherford / 1959 (Frankie Goes to Hollywood)

Jerry Butler / 1939 ("He Will Break Your Heart")

Phil Collen / 1957 (Def Leppard)

DECEMBER 9

Joan Armatrading / 1950 ("Drop the Pilot")

Rick Danko / 1943 (The Band)

Donny Osmond / 1957 (The Osmonds)

DECEMBER 10

Chad Stewart / 1943 (Chad & Jeremy)

Chris Kefford / 1946 (The Move)

DECEMBER 11

Booker T. Jones / 1944 (Booker T. & the MG's)

Brenda Lee / 1944 ("I'm Sorry")

David Gates / 1940 (Bread)

Nikki Six / 1958 (Motley Crue)

DECEMBER 12

Connie Francis / 1938 ("Where the Boys Are")

Dionne Warwick / 1940 ("Walk On By")

Sheila E. / 1959 ("Glamorous Life")

Cy Curnin / 1957 (The Fixx)

Dickey Betts / 1943 (The Allman Brothers Band)

Mike Pinder / 1942 (The Moody Blues)

Clive Bunker / 1946 (Jethro Tull)

Paul Rodgers / 1949 (Bad Company)

DECEMBER 13

Ted Nugent / 1948 ("Stranglehold")

Jeff "Skunk" Baxter / 1948 (The Doobie Brothers)

Berton Avere / 1954 (The Knack)

DECEMBER 14

Joyce Vincent / 1946 (Dawn)

Patty Duke / 1947 ("Don't Just Stand There")

Frank Allen / 1943 (The Searchers)

DECEMBER 15

Cindy Birdsong / 1939 (Patti LaBelle & the Bluebelles/replaced Florence
  Ballard in The Supremes)

Carmine Appice / 1946 (Vanilla Fudge)

Dave Clark / 1942 (The Dave Clark Five)

Paul Simonon / 1955 (The Clash)

DECEMBER 16

Billy Gibbons / 1949 (ZZ Top)

Benny Andersson / 1946 (ABBA)

Tony Hicks / 1943 (The Hollies)

DECEMBER 17

Eddie Kendricks / 1939 (The Temptations)

Jim Bonfanti / 1948 (The Raspberries)

Art Neville / 1937 (The Neville Brothers)

Paul Butterfield / 1942 (Paul Butterfield Blues Band)

Carlton Barrett / 1950 (Bob Marley & the Wailers)

DECEMBER 18

Keith Richards / 1943 (The Rolling Stones)

Chas Chandler / 1938 (The Animals)

DECEMBER 19

Zal Yanovsky / 1944 (The Lovin' Spoonful)

Maurice White / 1944 (Earth, Wind & Fire)

Alvin Lee / 1944 (Ten Years After)

DECEMBER 20

Bobby Colomby / 1944 (Blood, Sweat & Tears)

Alex Chilton / 1950 (Big Star)

Stevie Wright / 1948 (The Easybeats)

Billy Bragg / 1957 ("She's Leaving Home")

DECEMBER 21

Frank Zappa / 1940 (The Mothers of Invention)

Carl Wilson / 1946 (The Beach Boys)

Alan Freed / 1921 (pioneer rock promoter)

DECEMBER 22

Robin Gibb / 1949 (The Bee Gees)

Maurice Gibb / 1949 (The Bee Gees)

Rick Nielsen / 1946 (Cheap Trick)

DECEMBER 23

Jorma Kaukonen / 1940 (Jefferson Airplane/Hot Tuna)

Dave Murray / 1958 (Iron Maiden)

Ron Bushy / 1945 (Iron Butterfly)

Tim Hardin / 1941 ("If I Were a Carpenter")

DECEMBER 24

Lee Dorsey / 1924 ("Working in a Coal Mine")

Lemmy / 1945 (Motorhead)

Ian Burden / 1957 (The Human League)

DECEMBER 25

Little Richard / 1932 ("Tutti Frutti")

Annie Lennox / 1954 (Eurythmics)

Jimmy Buffett / 1946 ("Margaritaville")

O'Kelly Isley / 1937 (The Isley Brothers)

DECEMBER 26

Abdul "Duke" Fakir / 1935 (The Four Tops)

Phil Spector / 1940 (producer)

Gordon Edwards / 1946 (The Pretty Things)

DECEMBER 27

Peter Criss / 1947 (KISS)

Mick Jones / 1944 (Foreigner)

Larry Byrom / 1948 (Steppenwolf)

Les Maguire / 1941 (Gerry & the Pacemakers)

DECEMBER 28

Edgar Winter / 1946 ("Frankenstein")

Johnny Otis / 1921 ("Willie and the Hand Jive")

"Pops" Staples / 1915 (The Staple Singers)

Dick Diamonte / 1947 (The Easybeats)

Dorsey Burnette / 1932 ("Hey Little One")

DECEMBER 29

Marianne Faithful / 1946 ("As Tears Go By")

Ray Thomas / 1942 (The Moody Blues)

DECEMBER 30

Davy Jones / 1945 (The Monkees)

Mike Nesmith / 1942 (The Monkees)

Jeff Lynne / 1947 (Electric Light Orchestra/The Travelling Wilburys)

Del Shannon / 1939 ("Runaway")

Bo Diddley / 1928 ("Who Do You Love")

Patti Smith / 1946 ("Because the Night")

DECEMBER 31

Donna Summer / 1948 ("She Works Hard for the Money")

Burton Cummings / 1947 (Guess Who)

Andrew Summers / 1942 (The Police)

Tom Hamilton / 1951 (Aerosmith)

Hole: (*Left to right*) Kristen M. Pfaff, Penny Schemel, Courtney Love, Eric Erlandson

Every Pertinent Rock & Roll, Pop, and Soul Grammy Award Winner

Marvin Gaye in 1983, when his song "Sexual Healing" won him his first Grammy Award

RECORD OF THE YEAR

1994	"All I Wanna Do"—Sheryl Crow
1993	"I Will Always Love You"—Whitney Houston
1992	"Tears in Heaven"—Eric Clapton
1991	"Unforgettable"—Natalie Cole/Nat King Cole
1990	"Another Day in Paradise"—Phil Collins
1989	"The Wind Beneath My Wings"—Bette Midler

1988	"Don't Worry Be Happy"—Bobby McFerrin
1987	"Graceland"—Paul Simon
1986	"Higher Love"—Steve Winwood
1985	"We Are the World"—USA for Africa
1984	"What's Love Got to Do with It"—Tina Turner
1983	"Beat It"—Michael Jackson
1982	"Rosanna"—Toto
1981	"Bette Davis Eyes"—Kim Carnes
1980	"Sailing"—Christopher Cross
1979	"What a Fool Believes"—The Doobie Brothers
1978	"Just the Way You Are"—Billy Joel
1977	"Hotel California"—The Eagles
1976	"This Masquerade"—George Benson
1975	"Love Will Keep Us Together"—The Captain & Tennille
1974	"I Honestly Love You"—Olivia Newton-John
1973	"Killing Me Softly with His Song"—Roberta Flack
1972	"The First Time Ever I Saw Your Face"—Roberta Flack
1971	"It's Too Late"—Carole King
1970	"Bridge Over Troubled Water"—Simon & Garfunkel
1969	"Aquarius/Let the Sunshine In"—The Fifth Dimension
1968	"Mrs. Robinson"—Simon & Garfunkel
1967	"Up, Up and Away"—The Fifth Dimension
1966	"Strangers in the Night"—Frank Sinatra
1965	"A Taste of Honey"—Herb Alpert & the Tijuana Brass
1964	"The Girl from Ipanema"—Stan Getz and Astrid Gilberto
1963	"The Days of Wine and Roses"—Henry Mancini
1962	"I Left My Heart in San Francisco"—Tony Bennett
1961	"Moon River"—Henry Mancini
1960	"Theme from 'A Summer Place'"—Percy Faith
1959	"Mack the Knife"—Bobby Darin
1958	"Nel Blu Dipinto Di Blu (Volare)"—Domenico Modugno

The Doobie Brothers: *(Left to right)* Patrick Simmons, Jeff Baxter, Tommy Johnston, Michael McDonald, *(front row)* John Hartman, Tiran Porter, Keith Knudson

ALBUM OF THE YEAR

1994	*MTV—Unplugged* Tony Bennett
1993	*The Bodyguard* (soundtrack)—Whitney Houston and others
1992	*Unplugged*—Eric Clapton
1991	*Unforgettable*—Natalie Cole
1990	*Back on the Block*—Quincy Jones
1989	*Nick of Time*—Bonnie Raitt
1988	*Faith*—George Michael
1987	*The Joshua Tree*—U2
1986	*Graceland*—Paul Simon
1985	*No Jacket Required*—Phil Collins
1984	*Can't Slow Down*—Lionel Ritchie
1983	*Thriller*—Michael Jackson
1982	*Toto IV*—Toto
1981	*Double Fantasy*—John Lennon & Yoko Ono
1980	*Christopher Cross*—Christopher Cross
1979	*52nd Street*—Billy Joel

1978   *Saturday Night Fever* (soundtrack)—The Bee Gees
        and others

1977   *Rumours*—Fleetwood Mac

1976   *Songs in the Key of Life*—Stevie Wonder

1975   *Still Crazy After All These Years*—Paul Simon

1974   *Fulfillingness' First Finale*—Stevie Wonder

1973   *Innervisions*—Stevie Wonder

1972   *The Concert for Bangledesh*—George Harrison, Ringo
        Starr, Bob Dylan, Leon Russell, Ravi Shankar, Eric
        Clapton, Klaus Voorman, Billy Preston

1971   *Tapestry*—Carole King

1970   *Bridge Over Troubled Waters*—Simon & Garfunkel

1969   *Blood, Sweat & Tears*—Blood, Sweat & Tears

1968   *By the Time I Get to Phoenix*—Glen Campbell

1967   *Sgt. Pepper's Lonely Hearts Club Band*—The Beatles

1966   *Sinatra: A Man and His Music*—Frank Sinatra

1965   *September of My Years*—Frank Sinatra

1964   *Getz/Gilberto*—Stan Getz and Joao Gilberto

1963   *The Barbra Streisand Album*—Barbra Streisand

1962   *The First Family*—Vaughn Meader

1961   *Judy at Carnegie Hall*—Judy Garland

1960   *Button Down Mind*—Bob Newhart

1959   *Come Dance with Me*—Frank Sinatra

1958   *The Music from "Peter Gunn"*—Henry Mancini

SONG OF THE YEAR (SONGWRITERS' AWARD)

1994   "Streets of Philadelphia"—Bruce Springsteen

1993   "A Whole New World"—Alan Menken and Tim Rice

1992   "Tears in Heaven"—Eric Clapton and Will Jennings

1991   "Unforgettable"—Irving Gordon

1990   "From a Distance"—Julie Gold

1989   "Wind Beneath My Wings"—Larry Henley and Jeff Silber

1988   "Don't Worry Be Happy"—Bobby McFerrin

1987	"Somewhere Out There"—James Horner, Barry Mann, Cynthia Weil
1986	"That's What Friends Are For"—Burt Bacharach and Carole Bayer Sager
1985	"We Are the World"—Michael Jackson and Lionel Richie
1984	"What's Love Got to Do with It"—Graham Lyle and Terry Britten
1983	"Every Breath You Take"—Sting
1982	"Always on My Mind"—John Christopher, Mark James, Wayne Carson
1981	"Bette Davis Eyes"—Donna Weiss and Jackie DeShannon
1980	"Sailing"—Christopher Cross
1979	"What a Fool Believes"—Kenny Loggins and Michael McDonald
1978	"Just the Way You Are"—Billy Joel
1977	Tie: "Love Theme from 'A Star Is Born' (Evergreen)"—Barbra Streisand and Paul Williams; "You Light Up My Life"—Joe Brooks
1976	"I Write the Songs"—Bruce Johnson
1975	"Send in the Clowns"—Stephen Sondheim
1974	"The Way We Were"—Marilyn & Alan Bergman, Marvin Hamlish
1973	"Killing Me Softly with His Song"—Norman Gimbel and Charles Fox
1972	"The First Time Ever I Saw Your Face"—Ewan MacColl
1971	"You've Got a Friend"—Carole King
1970	"Bridge over Troubled Water"—Paul Simon
1969	"Games People Play"—Joe South
1968	"Little Green Apples"—Bobby Russell
1967	"Up, Up and Away"—Jim Webb
1966	"Michelle"—John Lennon and Paul McCartney
1965	"The Shadow of Your Smile"—Paul Francis Webster and Johnny Mandel
1964	"Hello Dolly"—Jerry Herman

1963	"The Days of Wine and Roses"—Henry Mancini and Johnny Mercer
1962	"What Kind of Fool Am I"—Leslie Bricuse and Anthony Newley
1961	"Moon River"—Henry Mancini and Johnny Mercer
1960	"Theme from 'Exodus' "—Ernest Gold
1959	"The Battle of New Orleans"—Jimmy Driftwood
1958	"Nel Blu Dipinto Di Blu (Volare)"—Domenico Mondugno

Cyndi Lauper

BEST NEW ARTIST

1994	Sheryl Crow
1993	Toni Braxton
1992	Arrested Development

1991	Marc Cohn
1990	Mariah Carey
1989	Milli Vanilli (later rescinded—see section on scandals,"Who's Zoomin' Who?")
1988	Tracy Chapman
1987	Jody Watley
1986	Bruce Hornsby & the Range
1985	Sade
1984	Cyndi Lauper
1983	Culture Club
1982	Men at Work
1981	Sheena Easton
1980	Christopher Cross
1979	Ricki Lee Jones
1978	A Taste of Honey
1977	Debby Boone
1976	Starland Vocal Band
1975	Natalie Cole
1974	Marvin Hamlisch
1973	Bette Midler
1972	America
1971	Carly Simon
1970	The Carpenters
1969	Crosby, Stills & Nash
1968	Jose Feliciano
1967	Bobbie Gentry
1966	no award given
1965	Tom Jones
1964	The Beatles
1963	The Swingle Singers
1962	Robert Goulet
1961	Bob Newhart
1960	Peter Nero
1959	Bobby Darin

POP VOCAL PERFORMANCE, FEMALE

1994	"All I Wanna Do"—Sheryl Crow
1993	"I Will Always Love You"—Whitney Houston
1992	"Constant Craving"—k.d. lang
1991	"Something to Talk About"—Bonnie Raitt
1990	"Vision of Love"—Mariah Carey
1989	"Nick of Time"—Bonnie Raitt
1988	"Fast Car"—Tracy Chapman
1987	"I Wanna Dance with Somebody (Who Loves Me)" —Whitney Houston
1986	*The Broadway Album*—Barbra Streisand
1985	"Saving All My Love for You"—Whitney Houston
1984	"What's Love Got to Do with It"—Tina Turner
1983	"Flashdance . . . What a Feeling"—Irene Cara
1982	"You Should Hear How She Talks About You" —Melissa Manchester
1981	"Lena Horne: The Lady and Her Music Live on Broadway"—Lena Horne
1980	"The Rose"—Bette Midler
1979	"I'll Never Love This Way Again"—Dionne Warwick
1978	"You Needed Me"—Anne Murray
1977	"Love Theme from 'A Star Is Born' (Evergreen)" —Barbra Streisand
1976	*Hasten Down the Wind*—Linda Ronstadt
1975	"At Seventeen"—Janis Ian
1974	"I Honestly Love You"—Olivia Newton-John
1973	"Killing Me Softly with His Song"—Roberta Flack
1972	"I Am Woman"—Helen Reddy
1971	*Tapestry*—Carole King
1970	"I'll Never Fall in Love Again"—Dionne Warwick
1969	"Is That All There Is"—Peggy Lee
1968	"Do You Know the Way to San Jose"—Dionne Warwick

1967	"Ode to Billie Joe"—Bobbie Gentry (also awarded Best Contemporary Vocal Performance, Female)
1966	"If He Walked into My Life"—Eydie Gorme
1965	"I Know a Place"—Petula Clark (also awarded Best Contemporary Vocal Performance, Female)
1965	*My Name Is Barbra*—Barbra Streisand
1964	"People"—Barbra Streisand
1963	*The Barbra Streisand Album*—Barbra Streisand
1962	*Ella Swings Brightly with Nelson Riddle*—Ella Fitzgerald
1961	*Judy at Carnegie Hall*—Judy Garland
1960	*Mack the Knife—Ella in Berlin*—Ella Fitzgerald (album category)
1960	"Mack the Knife"—Ella Fitzgerald (single category)
1959	"But Not for Me"—Ella Fitzgerald
1958	*The Irving Berlin Song Book*—Ella Fitzgerald

Barry Manilow

BEST POP VOCAL PERFORMANCE, MALE

1994	"Can You Feel the Love Tonight"—Elton John
1993	"If I Ever Lose My Faith in You"—Sting
1992	"Tears in Heaven"—Eric Clapton
1991	"When a Man Loves a Woman"—Michael Bolton
1990	"Oh Pretty Woman"—Roy Orbison
1989	"How Am I Supposed to Live Without You"—Michael Bolton
1988	"Don't Worry Be Happy"—Bobby McFerrin
1987	*Bring on the Night*—Sting
1986	"Higher Love"—Steve Winwood
1985	"No Jacket Required"—Phil Collins
1984	"Against All Odds (Take a Look at Me Now)"—Phil Collins
1983	*Thriller*—Michael Jackson
1982	"Truly"—Lionel Richie
1981	*Breakin' Away*—Al Jarreau
1980	"This Is It"—Kenny Loggins
1979	*52nd Street*—Billy Joel
1978	"Copacabana (At the Copa)"—Barry Manilow
1977	"Handy Man"—James Taylor
1976	*Songs in the Key of Life*—Stevie Wonder
1975	*Still Crazy After All These Years*—Paul Simon
1974	*Fulfillingness' First Finale*—Stevie Wonder
1973	"You Are the Sunshine of My Life"—Stevie Wonder
1972	"Without You"—Harry Nilsson
1971	"You've Got a Friend"—James Taylor
1970	"Everything Is Beautiful"—Ray Stevens
1969	"Everybody's Talkin'"—Harry Nilsson
1968	"Light My Fire"—Jose Feliciano
1967	"By the Time I Get to Phoenix"—Glen Campbell
1966	"Strangers in the Night"—Frank Sinatra
1965	"King of the Road"—Roger Miller (Best Contemporary Vocal Performance, Male)

1965	"It Was a Very Good Year"—Frank Sinatra
1964	"Hello, Dolly!"—Louis Armstrong
1963	"Wives and Lovers"—Jack Jones
1962	"I Left My Heart in San Francisco"—Tony Bennett
1961	"Lollipops and Roses"—Jack Jones
1960	*Genius of Ray Charles*—Ray Charles (album category)
1960	"Georgia on My Mind"—Ray Charles (single category)
1959	*Come Dance with Me*—Frank Sinatra
1958	"Catch a Falling Star"—Perry Como

The Pointer Sisters: *(Left to right)* June, Anita, and Ruth

BEST POP PERFORMANCE BY A DUO OR GROUP WITH VOCAL

1994	"I Swear"—All-4-One
1993	"A Whole New World (Aladdin's Theme)"—Peabo Bryson and Regina Bell
1992	"Beauty and the Beast"—Celine Dion and Peabo Bryson
1991	"Losing My Religion"—R.E.M.
1990	"All of My Life"—Linda Ronstadt and Aaron Neville
1989	"Don't Know Much"—Linda Ronstadt and Aaron Neville
1988	*Brasil*—The Manhattan Transfer
1987	"(I've Had) The Time of My Life"—Bill Medley and Jennifer Warnes
1986	"That's What Friends Are For"—Dionne Warwick & Friends, featuring Stevie Wonder, Elton John, Gladys Knight
1985	"We Are the World"—USA for Africa
1984	"Jump (for My Love)"—The Pointer Sisters
1983	"Every Breath You Take"—The Police
1982	"Up Where We Belong"—Joe Cocker and Jennifer Warnes
1981	"Boy from New York City"—The Manhattan Transfer
1980	"Guilty"—Barbra Streisand and Barry Gibb
1979	*Minute by Minute*—The Doobie Brothers
1978	*Saturday Night Fever*—The Bee Gees
1977	"How Deep Is Your Love"—The Bee Gees
1976	"If You Leave Me Now"—Chicago
1975	"Lyin' Eyes"—The Eagles
1974	"Band on the Run"—Paul McCartney & Wings
1973	"Neither One of Us (Wants to Be the First to Say Goodbye)"—Gladys Knight & the Pips
1972	"Where Is the Love"—Roberta Flack and Donny Hathaway
1971	*Carpenters*—The Carpenters
1970	"Close to You"—The Carpenters
1969	"Aquarius/Let the Sunshine In"—The Fifth Dimension

1968	"Mrs. Robinson"—Simon & Garfunkel
1967	"Up, Up and Away"—The Fifth Dimension
1966	"A Man and a Woman"—The Anita Kerr Singers
1965	*We Dig Mancini*—The Anita Kerr Singers
1964	*A Hard Day's Night*—The Beatles
1963	"Blowin' in the Wind"—Peter, Paul & Mary
1962	"If I Had a Hammer"—Peter, Paul & Mary
1961	*High Flying*—Lambert, Hendricks & Ross
1960	"We Got Us"—Eydie Gorme & Steve Lawrence
1959	"Battle Hymn of the Republic"—Mormon Tabernacle Choir
1958	"That Old Black Magic"—Louis Prima and Keely Smith

BEST POP ALBUM

| 1994 | *Longing in Their Hearts*—Bonnie Raitt |

BEST POP VOCAL COLLABORATION

| 1994 | "Funny How Time Slips Away"—Al Green and Lyle Lovett |

OTHER POP/ROCK & ROLL/ CONTEMPORARY AWARDS

1970	"Bridge Over Troubled Water"—Paul Simon as songwriter (Best Contemporary Song)
1969	"The Games People Play"—Joe South as songwriter (Best Contemporary Song)
1967	*Sgt. Pepper's Lonely Hearts Club Band*—The Beatles (Best Contemporary Album)
1967	"Up, Up and Away"—The Fifth Dimension (Best Contemporary Single)
1966	"Winchester Cathedral"—The New Vaudville Band (Best Contemporary Recording)

1966   "Eleanor Rigby"—Paul McCartney
        (Best Contemporary Solo Vocal)

1965   "Flowers on the Wall"—The Statler Brothers
        (Best Contemporary Group)

1965   "King of the Road"—Roger Miller
        (Best Contemporary Single)

1964   "Downtown"—Petula Clark (Best Rock & Roll Recording)

1963   "Deep Purple"—Nino Tempo & April Stevens
        (Best Rock & Roll Recording)

1962   "Alley Cat"—Bent Fabric (Best Rock & Roll Recording)

1961   "Let's Twist Again"—Chubby Checker
        (Best Rock & Roll Recording)

1960   "Georgia on My Mind"—Ray Charles (Best Pop Single)

1959   "Midnight Flyer"—Nat "King" Cole (Best Top 40)

Dionne Warwick in 1980 the same week she won two Grammy Awards

BEST ROCK VOCAL PERFORMANCE, FEMALE

1994	"Come to My Window"—Melissa Etheridge
1993	combined with Rock Male category this year
1992	"Ain't It Heavy"—Melissa Etheridge
1991	*Luck of the Draw*—Bonnie Raitt (Best Rock Vocal Performance, Solo)
1990	"Black Velvet"—Alannah Myles
1989	*Nick of Time*—Bonnie Raitt
1988	*Tina Live in Europe*—Tina Turner
1987	combined with Rock Male category this year
1986	"Back Where You Started"—Tina Turner
1985	"One of the Living"—Tina Turner
1984	"Better Be Good to Me"—Tina Turner
1983	"Love Is a Battlefield"—Pat Benatar
1982	"Shadows of the Night"—Pat Benatar
1981	"Fire and Ice"—Pat Benatar
1980	*Crimes of Passion*—Pat Benatar
1979	"Hot Stuff"—Donna Summer

BEST ROCK VOCAL PERFORMANCE, MALE

1994	"Streets of Philadelphia"—Bruce Springsteen
1993	"I'd Do Anything for Love (But I Won't Do That)" —Meatloaf
1992	*Unplugged*—Eric Clapton
1991	combined with Rock Female category this year
1990	"Bad Love"—Eric Clapton
1989	*The End of the Innocence*—Don Henley
1988	"Simply Irresistible"—Robert Palmer
1987	*Tunnel of Love*—Bruce Springsteen
1986	"Addicted to Love"—Robert Plamer
1985	"The Boys of Summer"—Don Henley
1984	"Dancing in the Dark"—Bruce Springsteen

1983	"Beat It"—Michael Jackson
1982	"Hurts So Good"—John Cougar
1981	"Jessie's Girl"—Rick Springfield
1980	*Glass Houses*—Billy Joel
1979	"Gotta Serve Somebody"—Bob Dylan

BEST ROCK PERFORMANCE BY A DUO OR GROUP WITH VOCAL

1994	"Crazy"—Aerosmith
1993	"Livin' on the Edge"—Aerosmith
1992	*Achtung Baby*—U2
1991	"Good Man, Good Woman"—Bonnie Raitt and Delbert McClinton
1990	"Janie's Got a Gun"—Aerosmith
1989	*Traveling Wilburys, Volume One* —The Traveling Wilburys
1988	"Desire"—U2
1987	*The Joshua Tree*—U2
1986	"Missionary Man"—Eurythmics
1985	"Money for Nothing"—Dire Straits
1984	*Purple Rain (Music from the Motion Picture)*—Prince
1983	*Synchronicity*—The Police
1982	"Eye of the Tiger"—Survivor
1981	"Don't Stand So Close to Me"—The Police
1980	*Against the Wind*—Bob Seger & the Silver Bullet Band
1979	"Heartache Tonight"—The Eagles

BEST ROCK INSTRUMENTAL PERFORMANCE

| 1994 | "Marooned"—Pink Floyd |
| 1993 | "Sofa"—Frank Zappa's Universe Rock Group, featuring Steve Vai |

1992	"Little Wing"—Stevie Ray Vaughan & Double Trouble
1991	"Cliffs of Dover"—Eric Johnson
1990	"D/FW"—The Vaughan Brothers
1989	*Jeff Beck's Guitar Shop with Terry Bozzio and Terry Hymas*—Jeff Beck, Terry Bozzio, Terry Hymas
1988	"Blues for Salvador"—Carlos Santana
1987	*Jazz from Hell*—Frank Zappa
1986	"Peter Gunn"—The Art of Noise, featuring Duane Eddy
1985	"Escape"—Jeff Beck
1984	"Cinema"—Yes
1983	"Brimstone and Treacle"—Sting
1982	"D.N.A."—A Flock of Seagulls
1981	"Behind My Camel"—The Police
1980	"Regatta de Blanc"—The Police
1979	"Rockestra"—Paul McCartney & Wings

BEST ROCK SONG (SONGWRITERS' AWARD)

1994	"Streets of Philadelphia"—Bruce Springsteen
1993	"Runaway Train"—David Pirner
1992	"Layla"—Eric Clapton and Jim Gordon
1991	"Soul Cages"—Sting

BEST ROCK ALBUM

1994	*Voodoo Lounge*—The Rolling Stones

BEST HARD ROCK/METAL PERFORMANCE

1988	*Crest of a Knave*—Jethro Tull

BEST HARD ROCK PERFORMANCE

1994	*Black Hole Sun*—Soundgarden
1993	*Plush*—Stone Temple Pilots

1991   *For Unlawful Carnal Knowledge*—Van Halen

1990   *Time's Up*—Living Colour

1989   "Cult of Personality"—Living Colour

BEST METAL PERFORMANCE

1994   "Spoonman"—Soundgarden

1993   Don't Want to Change the World"—Ozzy Osbourne

1992   "Wish"—Nine Inch Nails

1991   *Metallica*—Metallica

1990   "Stone Cold Crazy"—Metallica

1989   "One"—Metallica

BEST ALTERNATIVE MUSIC PERFORMANCE

1994   *Dookie*—Green Day

1993   *Zooropa*—U2

1992   *Bone Machine*—Tom Waits

1991   *Out of Time*—R.E.M.

1990   *I Do Not Want What I Haven't Got*—Sinead O'Connor

BEST RHYTHM & BLUES RECORDING

1967   "Respect"—Aretha Franklin

1966   "Crying Time"—Ray Charles

1965   "Papa's Got a Brand New Bag"—James Brown

1964   "How Glad I Am"—Nancy Wilson

1963   "Busted"—Ray Charles

1962   "I Can't Stop Loving You"—Ray Charles

1961   "Hit the Road Jack"—Ray Charles

1960   "Let the Good Times Roll"—Ray Charles

1959   "What a Difference a Day Makes"—Dinah Washington

1958   "Tequila"—The Champs

Aretha Franklin

BEST RHYTHM & BLUES VOCAL PERFORMANCE, FEMALE

1994	"Breathe Again"—Toni Braxton
1993	"Another Sad Love Song"—Toni Braxton
1992	*The Woman I Am*—Chaka Khan
1991	Tie: *I'm Burnin'*—Patti Labelle; "How Can I Ease the Pain"—Lisa Fischer
1990	*Compositions*—Anita Baker
1989	*Giving You the Best That I Got*—Anita Baker
1988	"Giving You the Best I Got"—Anita Baker
1987	*Aretha*—Aretha Franklin
1986	*Rapture*—Anita Baker
1985	"Freeway of Love"—Aretha Franklin

1984	"I Feel for You"—Chaka Khan
1983	*Chaka Khan*—Chaka Khan
1982	"And I Am Telling You I'm Not Going"—Jennifer Holliday
1981	"Hold On I'm Comin' "—Aretha Franklin
1980	"Never Knew Love Like This"—Stephanie Mills
1979	"Deja Vu"—Dionne Warwick
1978	"Last Dance"—Donna Summer
1977	"Don't Leave Me This Way"—Thelma Houston
1976	"Sophisticated Lady (She's a Different Lady)"—Natalie Cole
1975	"This Will Be"—Natalie Cole
1974	"Ain't Nothing Like the Real Thing"—Aretha Franklin
1973	"Master of Eyes"—Aretha Franklin
1972	*Young, Gifted and Black*—Aretha Franklin
1971	"Bridge Over Troubled Water"—Aretha Franklin
1970	"Don't Play That Song"—Aretha Franklin
1969	"Share Your Love with Me"—Aretha Franklin
1968	"Chain of Fools"—Aretha Franklin
1967	"Respect"—Aretha Franklin

BEST RHYTHM & BLUES VOCAL PERFORMANCE, MALE

1994	"When Can I See You"—Babyface
1993	"A Song for You"—Ray Charles
1992	*Heaven and Earth*—Al Jarreau
1991	*Power of Love*—Luther Vandross
1990	"Here and Now"—Luther Vandross
1989	"Every Little Step"—Bobby Brown
1988	*Introducing the Hardline According to Terrence Trent D'Arby*—Terrence Trent D'Arby
1987	"Just to See Her"—Smokey Robinson
1986	"Living in America"—James Brown
1985	*In Square Circle*—Stevie Wonder
1984	"Caribbean Queen (No More Love on the Run)"—Billy Ocean

Stevie Wonder

1983	"Billie Jean"—Michael Jackson
1982	"Sexual Healing"—Marvin Gaye
1981	"One Hundred Ways"—James Ingram
1980	*Give Me the Night*—George Benson
1979	"Don't Stop 'Til You Get Enough"—Michael Jackson
1978	"On Broadway"—George Benson
1977	*Unmistakably Lou*—Lou Rawls
1976	"I Wish"—Stevie Wonder
1975	"Living for the City"—Ray Charles
1974	"Boogie on Reggae Woman"—Stevie Wonder
1973	"Superstition"—Stevie Wonder

1972	"Me and Mrs. Jones"—Billy Paul
1971	"A Natural Man"—Lou Rawls
1970	"The Thrill Is Gone"—B.B. King
1969	"The Chokin' Kind"—Joe Simon
1968	"(Sittin' on) The Dock of the Bay"—Otis Redding
1967	"Dead End Street"—Lou Rawls
1966	"Crying Time"—Ray Charles

BEST RHYTHM & BLUES GROUP, VOCAL OR INSTRUMENTAL

1970	"Didn't I (Blow Your Mind This Time)"—The Delphonics
1969	"It's Your Thing"—The Isley Brothers
1968	"Cloud Nine"—The Temptations
1967	"Soul Man"—Sam & Dave
1966	"Hold It Right There"—The Ramsey Louis Trio

BEST RHYTHM & BLUES PERFORMANCE BY A DUO OR GROUP WITH VOCAL

1994	"I'll Make Love to You"—Boyz II Men
1993	"No Ordinary Love"—Sade
1992	"End of the Road"—Boyz II Men
1991	*Cooleyhighharmony*—Boyz II Men
1990	"I'll Be Good to You"—Ray Charles and Chaka Khan
1989	"Back to Life"—Soul II Soul featuring Caron Wheeler
1988	"Love Overboard"—Gladys Knight & the Pips
1987	"I Knew You Were Waiting for Me"—Aretha Franklin and George Michael
1986	"Kiss"—Prince & the Revolution
1985	"Nightshift"—The Commodores
1984	"Yah Mo B There"—James Ingram and Michael McDonald

Prince (or is that "formerly known as Prince"?)

1983	"Ain't Nobody"—Rufus & Chaka Khan
1982	Tie: "Let It Whip"—Dazz Band; "Wanna Be with You" —Earth, Wind & Fire
1981	*The Dude*—Quincy Jones
1980	"Shining Star"—The Manhattans
1979	"After the Love Is Gone"—Earth, Wind & Fire
1978	*All 'n' All*—Earth, Wind & Fire
1977	"Best of My Love"—The Emotions
1976	"You Don't Have to Be a Star (to Be in My Show)" —Marilyn McCoo and Billy Davis Jr.

1975	"Shining Star"—Earth, Wind & Fire
1974	"Tell Me Something Good"—Rufus
1973	"Midnight Train to Georgia"—Gladys Knight & the Pips
1972	"Papa Was a Rolling Stone"—The Temptations
1971	"Proud Mary"—Ike & Tina Turner

BEST RHYTHM & BLUES ALBUM

| 1994 | *II*—Boyz II Men |

BEST RHYTHM & BLUES INSTRUMENTAL PERFORMANCE

1992	*Doo Bop*—Miles Davis
1992	no award given
1991	no award given
1990	no award given
1989	"African Dance"—Soul II Soul
1988	"Light Years"—Chick Corea
1987	"Chicago Song"—David Sanborn
1986	"And You Know That"—Yellowjackets
1985	*Musician*—Ernie Watts
1984	*Sound-System*—Herbie Hancock
1983	"Rockit"—Herbie Hancock
1982	"Sexual Healing"—Marvin Gaye
1981	"All I Need Is You"—David Sanborn
1980	"On Broadway"—George Benson
1979	"Boogie Wonderland"—Earth, Wind & Fire
1978	"Runnin'"—Earth, Wind & Fire
1977	"Q"—Brothers Johnson
1976	"Theme from 'Good King Bad'"—George Benson
1975	"Fly, Robin, Fly"—Silver Convention
1974	"TSOP (The Sound of Philadelphia)"—MSFB
1973	"Hang On Sloopy"—The Ramsey Lewis Trio

1972   "Papa Was a Rolling Stone"—The Temptations

1969   "Games People Play"—King Curtis

Boz Scaggs

BEST RYHTHM & BLUES SONG (SONGWRITERS' AWARD)

1994   "I'll Make Love to You"—Babyface

1993   "That's the Way Love Goes"—Janet Jackson,
               James Harris III, Terry Lewis

1992   "End of the Road"—L.A. Reid, Babyface, Daryl Simmons

1991   "Power of Love/Love Power"—Luther Vandross,
               Marcus Miller, Teddy Vann

1990   "U Can't Touch This"—Rick James, Alonzo Miller,
               M.C. Hammer

1989   "If You Don't Know Me by Now"—Kenny Gamble
               and Leon Huff

1988	Giving You the Best That I Got"—Anita Baker, Skip Scarborough, Randy Holland
1987	"Lean on Me"—Bill Withers
1986	"Sweet Love"—Anita Baker, Louis A. Johnson, Gary Bias
1985	"Freeway of Love"—Narada Michael Walden and Jeffrey Cohen
1984	"I Feel for You"—Prince
1983	"Billie Jean"—Michael Jackson
1982	"Turn Your Love Around"—Jay Graydon, Steve Lukather, Bill Champlin
1981	"Just the Two of Us"—Bill Withers, William Salter, Ralph MacDonald
1980	"Never Knew Love Like This Before"—Reggie Lucas and James Mtume
1979	"After the Love Is Gone"—David Foster, Jay Graydon, Bill Champlin
1978	"Last Dance"—Paul Jabara
1977	"You Make Me Feel Like Dancing"—Leo Sayer and Vini Poncia
1976	"Lowdown"—Boz Scaggs and David Paich
1975	"Where Is the Love"—Harry Wayne Casey, Richard Finch, Willie Clark, Betty Wright
1974	"Living for the City"—Stevie Wonder
1973	"Superstition"—Stevie Wonder
1972	"Papa Was a Rolling Stone"—Barrett Strong and Norman Whitfield
1971	"Ain't No Sunshine"—Bill Withers
1970	"Patches"—Ronald Dunbar and General Johnson
1969	"Color Him Father"—Richard Spencer
1968	"(Sittin' on) The Dock of the Bay"—Otis Redding and Steve Cropper

BEST DISCO RECORDING

| 1979 | "I Will Survive"—Gloria Gaynor |

A Rock & Roll Trivia Quiz

Appearing over the title of each section in this book is the title of a famous rock song in quotes.

- Who sang the original rock songs named over each of the titles found listed in this book's table of contents?

There are five exceptions on that list: "You Say It's Your Birthday," "Keeping Their Faces in a Jar by the Door," "One Is the Loneliest Number," and "Say the Word" are paraphrased from four famous rock songs.

- What are the actual song titles?
- Who recorded the songs?

Also:

- "I'm Gonna Hurl" is a phrase from a favorite rock & roll–oriented film. What is the film?
- What classic rock song was the hit of the above movie's soundtrack album?

The answers to this trivia quiz appear on pages 297–303 of this book.

Answers to the Rock & Roll Trivia Quiz

1 "Paperback Writer"

The Beatles (1966) [Number 1 hit single]

2 "Reflections"

The Supremes (1967) [Number 2 hit single]

3 "Rock 'n' Roll Is Here to Stay"

Danny & the Juniors (1958) [Number 19 hit single]

4 "Little Bit o' Soul"

Music Explosion (1967) [Number 2 hit single]

5 "Act Naturally"

The Beatles (1965) [lead vocal by Ringo Starr, the flip side of "Yesterday," "Act Naturally" hit Number 47 on the singles chart]

6 *"Lookin' Out for Number One"*

Bachman-Turner Overdrive (1976) [Number 65 hit single]

7 *"The Chapel of Love"*

The Dixie Cups (1964) [Number 1 hit single]

Bette Midler (1971) [from *The Divine Miss M* album]

8 *"Beautiful People"*

Melanie (1970) [from her *Candles in the Rain* album]

The New Seekers (1971) [Number 67 hit single]

9 *"Overnight Sensation"*

The Raspberries (1974) [Number 18 hit]

10 *"Dance Party"*

Martha & the Vandellas (1965) [title track to their
album of the same name]

11 *"At the Concert"*

Roberta Flack and Michael Henderson (1978) [from his *Goin' Places*
album]

12 *"Cover Me"*

Bruce Springsteen (1984) [Number 7 hit single]

13 *"Telephone Line"*

The Electric Light Orchestra (1977) [Number 7 hit single]

14 *"Hit the Road, Jack"*

Ray Charles (1961) [Number 1 hit single]

15 *"Colour My World"*

Chicago (1971) [flip side of "Beginnings" single]

16 *"Count Me In"*

Gary Lewis & the Playboys (1965) [Number 2 hit single]

17 *"Tutti Frutti"*

Little Richard (1956) [Number 17 hit single]

18 *"Go Where You Wanna Go"*

The Mamas & the Papas (1965) [cut from their album *If You Can Believe Your Eyes and Ears*]

The Fifth Dimension (1967) [Number 16 hit single]

19 *"Get a Job"*

The Silhouettes (1958) [Number 1 hit single]

20 *"Stairway to Heaven"*

Led Zeppelin (1971) [cut from their fourth, untitled album]

21 *"Die Young, Stay Pretty"*

Blondie (1979) [cut from their *Eat to the Beat* album]

Bob Seger

22 *"I'm Gonna Hurl"*

Term for vomiting taken from the film *Wayne's World* (1992)

The film's soundtrack revived Queen's 1976/Number 9 hit single "Bohemian Rhapsody"

23 *"Walk on the Wild Side"*

Lou Reed (1973) [Number 16 hit single]

24 *"Keeping Their Faces in a Jar by the Door"*

Paraphrased from The Beatles' song "Eleanor Rigby" (1966) [Number 11 hit single]

25 *"Kind of a Drag"*

The Buckinghams (1966) [Number 1 hit single]

26 *"Who's Zoomin' Who?"*

Aretha Franklin (1985) [Number 7 hit single]

27 *"Drive My Car"*

The Beatles (1965) [album cut from *Rubber Soul*]

28 *"Turn the Page"*

Bob Seger (1973) [album cut from *Back in '72*]

29 *"One Is the Loneliest Number"*

"One" is the actual title of the song, recorded by Three Dog Night (1969) [Number 5 hit single]

30 *"At the Zoo"*

Simon & Garfunkel (1967) [Number 16 hit single]

31 *"The Name Game"*

Shirley Ellis (1965) [Number 3 hit single]

LaBelle: *(Left to right)* Nona Hendryx, Patti LaBelle, Sarah Dash

32 *"Dancing Days"*

Led Zeppelin (1973) [cut from their *Houses of the Holy* album]

33 *"Jazzman"*

Carole King (1974) [Number 2 hit single]

34 *"Wipe Out"*

The Safaris (1963) [Number 2 hit single]

35 *"Spooky"*

The Classics IV (1967) [Number 3 hit single]

36 *"Lucy in the Sky with Diamonds"*

The Beatles (1967) [album cut from *Sgt. Pepper's Lonely Hearts Club Band*]

37 *"We Are the Champions"*

Queen (1977) [Number 4 hit single]

38 *"You Say It's Your Birthday"*

The song title is "Birthday" by the Beatles (1968) [album cut from *The Beatles* a.k.a. The White Album]

39 *"I'm Winning"*

Nona Hendryx (1977) [cut from her album *Nona Hendryx*]

The Beatles

40 *"Love, Guess Who"*

Martha & the Vandellas (1970) [cut from their
album *Natural Resources*]

41 *"Say the Word"*

From the song "The Word" by The Beatles (1965) [cut from their
album *Rubber Soul*]

Photo Credits

Photos in this book were either taken by Mark Bego, or provided by the MJB Photo Archives. In the order of appearance in the book, the Archive photos are courtesy of the following record, management, or film companies:

The Beatles (Capitol Records), James Brown (Epic/Portrait Records), Carole King (Capitol Records), Elvis movie still (MGM Pictures), Whitney Houston (Arista Records), Michael Jackson (Epic Records), Cher (Casablanca Records), The Captain & Tennille (A&M Records), Patti Smith (Arista Records), Village People (David Fishof Productions), Gladys Knight & the Pips (Buddah/Arista Records), Jackson Browne (Asylum Records), The B-52's (Warner Brothers Records), Eric Carmen (Arista Records), America (Warner Brothers Records), Pat Benatar (Chrysalis Records), Eurythmics (Arista Records), The Who (MCA Records), The Carpenters (A&M Records), The Temptations (Atlantic Records), Indigo Girls/Melissa Etheridge (Epic Records), Kiss (Casablanca Records), Pete Burns/Dead or Alive (Epic Records), David Bowie (RCA Records), Madonna (Sire Records), Hall & Oates (RCA Records), Debbie Gibson (Atlantic Records), Connie Francis (MGM/Polydor Records), The Police (A&M Records), Cat Stevens (A&M Records), Three Dog Night (Dunhill/ABC Records), Rod Stewart (Warner Brothers Records), Blondie (Private Stock Records), Carly Simon (Warner Brothers Records), Sade (Epic Records), The Bee Gees (RSO Records), Simon &

Garfunkel (Warner Brothers Records), The Beatles (Capitol Records), Crosby/Stills/Nash/Young (Atlantic Records), Fleetwood Mac (Warner Brothers Records), Aretha Franklin (Atlantic Records), Elton John (MCA Records), Madonna (Sire Records), Joni Mitchell (Asylum Records), The Monkees (Colgems Records), Elvis Presley (RCA Records), Bonnie Raitt (Warner Brothers Records), Martha & the Vandellas (Motown Records), The Rolling Stones (Atlantic Records), The Supremes (Motown Records), Tina Turner (Capitol Records), Kenny Loggins (Columbia Records), James Taylor (Columbia Records), Peter Frampton (A&M Records), Rita Coolidge (Attic Records), The Four Tops (Arista Records), Culture Club (Epic/Virgin Records), Ashford & Simpson (Capitol Records), Joan Jett (Blackheart/Epic Records), Yes (Anderson Bruford Wakeman Howe) (Arista Records), Bette Midler (Atlantic Records), Marvin Gaye (Columbia Records), The Doobie Brothers (Warner Brothers Records), Cyndi Lauper (Portrait Records), Barry Manilow (Arista Records), The Pointer Sisters (Planet Records), Aretha Franklin (Arista Records), Stevie Wonder (Tamla Records), Prince (Warner Brothers Records), Boz Scaggs (Columbia Records), Bob Seger (Capitol Records), LaBelle (Epic Records), The Beatles (Capitol Records).

The following photos (in order of appearance) were taken by Mark Bego:

Rhythm & Blues Foundation ensemble (Mary Wilson, Inez Foxx, Bonnie Raitt, Fats Domino, Little Richard, Lloyd Price, Martha Reeves, Charlie Foxx, Katherine Anderson) at the Universal Hilton, Los Angeles; Crosby, Stills & Nash in concert at the Tucson Convention Center in Tucson, Arizona; Melanie in concert in Bethel, New York; Mary Wilson and Fred Schneider at the Palace Theater, Los Angeles; Bonnie Raitt and Martha Reeves at the Universal Hilton, Los Angeles; Dionne Warwick in her dressing room at the Westchester Theater, Tarrytown, New York.

Mark Bego

Mark Bego is the author of several best-selling books on rock & roll and show business, and with twenty-five books published and over 8 million books in print, he is "the best-selling biographer in the rock and pop music field." Heralded in the press as "the Prince of Pop Music Bios," he also has several new projects in the works.

His 1995 books, *I Fall to Pieces: The Music and the Life of Patsy Cline* (Adams Media Corp.) and *Bonnie Raitt: Just in the Nick of Time* (Carol Publishing), told the life stories of two of the most admired female singers in the country and rock world. Mark's *Alan Jackson* (1996/Taylor Publishing) tells of the rise of Nashville's hottest singer/songwriter.

In 1994 he collaborated with Martha Reeves of Martha & the Vandellas on her autobiography, *Dancing in the Street: Confessions of a Motown Diva*, and the book spent five weeks in the Top Ten of *The Chicago Tribune* best-seller list! The sizzling story of Martha's million-selling career with Motown Records—and beyond—this fascinating book takes the reader on an exciting roller coaster ride behind the scenes with one of the '60s' most beloved singers. It was released in August of 1994 by Hyperion Books/Disney Corporation.

Bego and Reeves embarked on a fourteen-city tour to promote the book in August and September 1994. *Publisher's Weekly* proclaimed the book "Poignant! . . . Reeves here recounts both the excitement and the energy of Motown in its heyday . . . she emerges as a stoic and likable survivor!"

In 1994, Pinnacle Books published his book *Country Gals*—featuring the likes of Reba McEntire, Wynonna Judd, and a dozen more of the hottest women on today's country scene. Also in June 1994, Contemporary Books released *Country Hunks*, the companion book to *Gals*, also by Mark. It features Garth Brooks, Alan Jackson, Clint Black, Vince Gill, Billy Ray Cyrus, and the most fascinating male stars of '90s' country music.

Mark worked with Micky Dolenz of The Monkees on Dolenz' autobiography, *I'm a Believer*. It was published in September 1993 by Hyperion Books, a division of Disney Corporation. The book traces Dolenz's life and career from "Circus Boy" in the 1950s through the three-decade Monkees saga, to his present solo career.

In June of 1992, Harmony Books/Random House published Mark's biography *Madonna: Blonde Ambition*, which is based on his interviews with Madonna and several of her intimate friends. Swept up into the controversy of Madonna's *Sex* book, Mark appeared on several national television talk shows, discussing his book and the whole Madonna phenomenon. In 1992 he was seen on "The Joan Rivers Show," "Maury Povich," "Hard Copy," "Faith Daniels," and "Entertainment Tonight." Bego is the on-camera host of the 1993 hour-long biographical video cassette entitled "Madonna: The Name of the Game," and he is also featured in A&E TV network's "Biography" special on Madonna.

In 1991 Mark Bego published his collaboration with Jimmy Greenspoon of Three Dog Night, *One Is the Loneliest Number* (Pharos Books), and worked with Vanilla Ice to write *Ice Ice Ice: The Extraordinary Vanilla Ice* (Dell). The Vanilla Ice book sold over half a million copies.

In 1989, Bego paired with teenage singing star Debbie Gibson. Together they wrote her biographical book, *Between The Lines* (1989). His Michael Jackson biography, *Michael!* (1984), spent six weeks on *The New York Times* best-seller list and sold over three million copies in six different languages. His other books have included the biographies *Linda Ronstadt: It's So Easy* (1990), *Aretha Franklin: Queen of Soul* (1989), *Bette Midler: Outrageously Divine* (1987), *Cher!* (1986), *Whitney!* [Houston] (1986), *Julian Lennon!* (1986), *Sade!* (1986), *Madonna!* (1985), *On the Road with Michael!* [Jackson] (1984), *The Doobie Brothers* (1980), *Barry Manilow* (1977), and *The Captain & Tennille* (1977).

Bego's books have also encompassed several other entertainment industry subjects. He has written about television: *TV Rock [The History of Rock & Roll on Television]* (1988) and *The Linda Gray Story*

(1988)—and the movies: *The Best of Modern Screen* (1986) and *Rock Hudson: Public & Private* (1986).

Reviewing Bego's *Madonna: Blonde Ambition*, social critic Camille Paglia devoted an entire chapter of the book to Mark's study of "the Material Girl." In it she wrote: "The strongest of several biographies is by Mark Bego, *Madonna: Blonde Ambition*. Bego is the author of more than twenty celebrity biographies, many of whose subjects have been singers—among them Barry Manilow, Michael Jackson, Whitney Houston, Cher, Bette Midler, and Aretha Franklin. *Madonna: Blonde Ambition* profits from his deep familiarity with the modern music industry, whose commercial dynamic he understands without condemning or excusing it."

Mark's writing has appeared in several magazines including *People, Us, The Star, Celebrity, Cosmopolitan, Penthouse, The Music Connection, Billboard*, and *The National Enguirer*. For two years Mark was the Nightlife Editor of *Cue* magazine in New York City, and from 1983–1985 he was the Editor-in-Chief of *Modern Screen* magazine. During 1992–1993, Bego resumed his magazine editing with "The Complete History of Madonna" and "The Complete History of Elvis Presley" for Sterlings/MacFadden Magazines. He frequently appears on radio and television, talking about the lives and careers of the stars. In 1990, Bego assisted Mary Wilson of The Supremes in editing and writing her autobiographical book, *Supreme Faith: Someday We'll Be Together*. Mark Bego divides his time between New York City; Los Angeles; and Tucson, Arizona.

Bego is currently working on his first novel, in collaboration with Mary Wilson. About the music industry, it is entitled *Motor City*.